THE NUCLEAR MENTALITY

THE NUCLEAR MENTALITY

A Psychosocial Analysis of the Arms Race

EDITED BY LYNN BARNETT AND IAN LEE

PLUTO  PRESS

in association with the
Medical Campaign against Nuclear Weapons
and the Study Group on
Psychosocial Issues in the Nuclear Age

First published 1989 by Pluto Press
345 Archway Road
London N6 5AA
and 8 Winchester Place, Winchester
MA 01890, USA

in association with the
Medical Campaign Against Nuclear Weapons
601 Holloway Road
London N19 4DJ

British Library Cataloguing in Publication Data
The nuclear mentality: a psychosocial analysis of the arms race
 1. Nuclear warfare. Psychological aspects
 I. Barnett, Lynn   II. Lee, Ian
 355'.0217

 ISBN 0–7453–0392–7
 ISBN 0–7453–0393–5 Pbk

Printed and bound in the UK by Billing & Sons Ltd, Worcester

Peace is abroad. But the arms race continues. Why?

Contents

Contributors

Lynn Barnett is Chair of the Study Group on Psychosocial Issues in the Nuclear Age and is a social scientist and child psychotherapist. She was trained and worked as a psychologist and social worker in Australia and as a social anthropologist in New Guinea, Crete and London before further training in child psychotherapy at the Tavistock Clinic. She works in this capacity in Exeter and lectures in child development and psychoanalytic theory at Exeter University. Author of several books, Lynn Barnett is currently making a cross-cultural video series on infant and child development.

Frank Barnaby was Director of the Stockholm International Peace Research Institute 1971–81, and since then has been visiting Professor at the Free University of Amsterdam and University of Minne-sota. Dr Barnaby worked as a nuclear physicist at the Atomic Weapons Research Establishment, Aldermaston, before joining the Medical Research Council's senior scientific staff and lecturing at the University of London. Dr Barnaby is the author of many papers on defence- and nuclear-related issues .

Norman Dixon retired in 1987 as Emeritus Professor and Research Fellow at University College, London. He lectures regularly to army, navy and civil defence colleges on stress, leadership and decision-making. Professor Dixon served in the Royal Engineers (in bomb disposal) 1940–50, and has published many books and papers: *Subliminal Perception and the Nature of Controversy* (McGraw Hill, 1971), *The Psychology of Military Incompetence* (Cape, 1976), *Preconscious Processing* (Wiley, 1981), and *Our Own Worst Enemy* (Cape, 1987).

Anton Obholzer has been chairman of the Tavistock Clinic for the past five years. His training is in psychiatry and psychoanalysis. Dr Obholzer's particular interest is in the application of psychoanalytic ideas to organisations and society at large.

Hanna Segal is co-founder of Psychoanalysts for the Prevention of Nuclear War, and of International Psychoanalysts Against Nuclear Weapons. She was Freud Visiting Professor at University College, London (1977–8) and trained at the Institute of Psychoanalysis where she was, variously, Scientific Secretary, Chair of the Education Committee, and President. Dr Segal qualified in medicine at the Polish Medical School, Edinburgh, in 1943 and is the author of numerous papers and several books including *Introduction to the Work of Melanie Klein* (Heinemann, 1964) and *The Work of Hanna Segal: a Kleinian Approach to Clinical Practice* (Free Association Books, 1986).

Morris Bradley is Co-Director of the Richardson Institute for Conflict and Peace Research and lectures in the Department of Psychiatry, University of Strathclyde. Dr Bradley studied biological psychology at the University of London. The Richardson Institute at the University of Lancaster provides postgraduate teaching and research on peace-related issues.

John Eldridge is Professor of Sociology at the University of Glasgow and a member of the Glasgow Media Group which has studied media reporting of nuclear- and defence-related issues, including several publications including *War and Peace News* (OUP, 1985).

The Oxford Research Group is an independent organisation funded by charitable trusts. Its purpose is to research how decisions are made on nuclear weapons in Britain, the USA, the USSR, France and China. **Scilla Elworthy** is Director of the Oxford Research Group, and a Research Fellow of the University of Bradford. She edited *How Nuclear Weapons Decisions Are Made* (Macmillan, 1986) under the name McLean, and is author of *Who Decides? Accountability and Nuclear Weapons Decision-Making in Britain* (Oxford, 1987). At the MCANW Conference she presented the paper on which Chapter 7 is based. The paper was written by **John Hamwee**, a senior lecturer at the Open University and Senior Research Fellow of the Oxford Research Group. **Hugh Miall**, who collaborated in the research for Chapter 7, is Research Director of the Oxford Research Group and his most recent publication is *Nuclear Weapons: Who's In Charge?* (Macmillan, 1987).

Ruth Davies trained as a psychologist and teacher; she is now a researcher at the Richardson Institute for Conflict and Peace Research, University of Lancaster.

Alastair Mackie retired prematurely as Director of Air Staff Briefing in the Ministry of Defence through profound disagreement with the direction of British and NATO nuclear weapons policies. He is now a Vice-Chair of the Campaign for Nuclear Disarmament, and a member of Ex-Services CND, Just Defence, Generals for Peace and Disarmament, and the London International Centre for Peacebuilding. Air Commodore Mackie served in the Royal Air Force for 26 years and taught service officers and civil servants about nuclear strategy and British defence policy at the Joint Services Staff College. On secondment to the Cabinet Office he was secretary to various committees and working parties dealing with NATO and Warsaw Pact strategies before becoming Director of Air Staff Briefing and, later, resigning.

Valentin Fomichev is a graduate of Moscow University International Law Department, and of the Diplomatic Academy. He is currently based at the Soviet Embassy in London.

Edy J. Korthals Altes resigned in July 1986 in protest at the direction of US and NATO nuclear policy, prompted by the dangers of SDI ('Star-Wars'). Drs Korthals Altes was previously Dutch Ambassador in Madrid and Warsaw, Head of Foreign Service in The Hague, and Deputy Permanent Representative to the Permanent Mission to the European Community in Brussels. He graduated in 1950 from the Rotterdam School of Economics. Now he is Vice-Chair of the Netherlands Pugwash Group and active in campaigning for peace and security in East–West relations. Drs Korthals Altes has published two books: *Man or Marionet* (Balans, 1987) and *An Emperor Without Clothes: an Outdated Security Policy* (Kok, 1988); he also writes frequently in leading Dutch newspapers.

Armorer Wason studied Russian at Cambridge University before working as a translator and editor with Progress Publishers in Moscow 1980–1. She trained and worked as a social worker and counsellor, mainly with young people, in London and later in Seattle, USA. She is now a consultant to organisations working in USSR and facilitates East–West exchanges.

Ian Munro joined the editorial staff of the *Lancet* in 1952, seven

years after qualifying in medicine at Guy's Hospital, London, and
was Editor 1976–88. Dr Munro is now Chairman of the UK–USSR
Medical Exchange Programme and Vice-Chair of the Medical Campaign Against Nuclear Weapons.

Ian Lee worked as a medical journalist and editor, before becoming
a peace activist involved mainly in the CruiseWatch and Interhelp
networks.

Preface and Acknowledgements

The Nuclear Mentality is based upon the National Conference of the Medical Campaign Against Nuclear Weapons (MCANW) organised by the Study Group on Psychosocial Issues in the Nuclear Age (SPINA), held on 22–3 April 1989 at the Royal College of Nursing, London. The Conference theme 'Peace is abroad. But the arms race continues. Why?' was prompted by two phenomena: the resistance of many political leaders to any change in the policies of nuclear war-fighting and first-use which the nuclear arsenals are intended to implement (despite headline-catching adjustments in the numbers of these weapons); and the failure so far of those favouring international cooperation instead of confrontation to alter this nuclear status quo, despite opinion polls over many years showing substantial public rejection of nuclear weapons policies in professedly democratic countries.

Urgency was added by evidence of an escalation in the nuclear arms race by NATO and the USA at a time when President Gorbachev's USSR appeared to be offering unprecedented opportunities to base international security on less wasteful and dangerous policies. Thus the Conference was entitled *The Nuclear Mentality – Dynamics and Change.*

MCANW brought a defence expert, a defence researcher, a media specialist, a Russian spokesman, a senior diplomat and a senior military man (both now retired), together with psychiatrists, psychoanalysts, psychotherapists and psychologists to examine what are the hidden forces which have made 'the unacceptable' so acceptable, even welcome to some people. Over 150 members of the medical profession attended the Conference, contributing to workshops and extended discussion periods. This publication incorporates their contributions with fuller versions of the papers presented to the Conference, and much additional material; edited discussion follows some of the chapters. Despite the inevitable unevenness of such a compilation, this carries forward the existing literature[32, 53, 56, 59–61, 65] on the psychological dimension of the

nuclear threat, and indicates a growing recognition of its importance. (Where other works are referred to in the text, full details are
listed alphabetically by author in the final chapter entitled Refer-
ences and Further Reading, and numbered accordingly; it is this
number which appears in superscript in the text, as above. V1, V2
and V3 refer to videos, listed on p. 176).

The Medical Campaign Against Nuclear Weapons is an association of health-care workers (doctors, nurses, psychologists,
administrators, laboratory technicians, social workers, therapists,
students and others) who agree that nuclear weapons pose the
greatest threat to human health and welfare. MCANW members
believe that preventing nuclear war is the only possible way to
protect people from its medical consequences. MCANW was
founded in 1980, and has around 4,000 members and 49 local
branches in Britain serviced by a national office at 601 Holloway
Rd, London N19 4DJ (tel. 01 272 2020).

President of MCANW is Sir Raymond Hoffenberg who was for-
merly President of the Royal College of Physicians. Emeritus
Professor David Morley, Institute of Child Health, University of
London, Dr Ian Munro (former Editor of the *Lancet*), Professor
Lesley Rees (Dean Elect of St Bartholomew's Hospital) and Professor
Barbara Tizard (Director of the Thomas Coram Research Institute,
University of London) are Vice-Presidents of MCANW.

The Study Group on Psychosocial Issues (SPINA) is a research and
educational group established in 1987 under MCANW auspices.
SPINA brings together the skills of psychologists, psychiatrists, psychotherapists, psychoanalysts and other professionals who are
concerned about the psychosocial causes and effects of the nuclear
arms race, and who hope to promote new ways of thinking about
international relations. The Conference on which this publication
is based was initiated by SPINA.

Thanks are due to the Westcroft Trust, Cambridge University Disarmament Seminar and the Medical Educational Trust for financial
help in research and publication. Thanks are also due for assistance
with research and its planning to Jill Hodges, Heather Hunt,
Michael Orgel and Barbara Tizard. For planning and organising the
Conference we are grateful to Tharu Naidoo, Gillian Reeve and
other SPINA members; finally, thanks are due to all the contributors to this book.

Introduction:
What is the Nuclear Mentality?

LYNN BARNETT

The nuclear arms race (and the nuclear mentality which supports it) is the world's 'most urgent health problem'.[42] If we do not learn how to deal with it we may never have the opportunity to treat any other problem.

But the psychological causes and consequences of the nuclear issue are so neglected that the initial reaction of many people may be – what is this 'nuclear mentality', and why is it so important? Is it urgent? It is urgent because today, in 1989, the risk of nuclear conflict and holocaust recognised over several decades is actually increasing – not decreasing as the Western media-focus on arms talks leads us to believe. This is shown in Chapter 1 by Dr Frank Barnaby.

The nuclear mentality is based on the belief that only the possession of and threat to use nuclear weapons will maintain peace in the world. The remaining chapters describe the dangerous elements of this mentality, and its resistance to change and popular opinion. One important focus is the adverse effects of the nuclear mentality upon us all now, whether or not in the future nuclear weapons policies do produce a nuclear conflict. Some insights as to how the nuclear mentality can be broken down are also offered.

Psychological knowledge is being applied in several countries to define and counteract the nuclear mentality. As two American psychiatrists,[42] members of US Physicians for Social Responsibility, put it: 'We must examine what forces produce flawed and dangerous thinking, what forces allow such thinking to be accepted unchallenged by the public and how we, as agents of change, can treat these problems ...'

These were the questions also identified by SPINA, the Study Group on Psychosocial Issues in the Nuclear Age, which is part of the Medical Campaign Against Nuclear Weapons. To start answering these fundamental and neglected questions SPINA and MCANW invited psychologists, psychiatrists, psychoanalysts, psychotherapists and other health workers to confer with a defence

1

expert, a defence researcher, a media specialist, a Russian spokesman, a senior diplomat and a senior military man at a two-day conference *The Nuclear Mentality – Dynamics and Change* in April 1989 at the Royal College of Nursing in London.

Simply increasing people's level of knowledge about the appalling consequences of nuclear war and the nuclear winter actually increases levels of anxiety and fear, leading often not to a more active response but to the strengthening of various defence mechanisms which keep the reality of that knowledge and fear at bay – non-productive mechanisms such as apathy, feelings of individual helplessness, denial, cynicism and so forth.

One other factor which handicaps individuals taking responsibility for the present terrifying situation and seeking, with others, to change it, is the complexity of the issues involved. This complexity, requiring the expertise of many disciplines, is reflected in the multidisciplinary membership of SPINA. Professor Robert Hinde,[52] a founder member of SPINA and head of the Medical Research Council Unit on the Development and Integration of Behaviour, at Cambridge University, has said:

> ... biology, psychology and the social sciences have important contributions to make to world peace as well as to the health and happiness of individuals. However, isolated endeavours are inadequate if those contributions are to be realized. The basic propensities with which man has been endowed; the properties of social interactions, relationships and groups; the beliefs, values and institutions of societies; and the dialectical relations between all of those, must all be tackled in an integrative way in order to meet the problems that confront us.

To do this, the broad range of knowledge assembled here to examine the nuclear mentality has focussed on four aspects:

First, what is the current situation with world nuclear arsenals, in which direction are weapons and policies being developed, and what are the risks of nuclear conflict?

Secondly, as psychologists and other child experts, we feel there is a crucial link between the nuclear mentality and early childhood experiences and child-rearing.

Thirdly, what group, institutional and individual processes support the maladaptive nuclear war mentality? And what can be done about them?

Fourthly, do the basic assumptions of those in positions of

power, particularly in relation to defence and armaments, show such maladaptive thinking and behaviour? Can organisations such as MCANW effect change here?

World Nuclear Arsenals, Current and Projected

Chapter 1, 'The Nuclear Arms Race: Running Hard' is essential first reading, because here Dr Frank Barnaby reveals the causes for alarm and suggests some corrective action by detailing the current state of world nuclear arsenals and the more dangerous direction in which weapons and policies are now developing.

Dr Barnaby explains how nuclear deterrence has involved each country's civilian population being treated as hostages under a permanent threat of nuclear extinction:

> NATO says that its nuclear strategy is one of nuclear deterrence based on assured destruction. Because the Soviets have similar strategic capabilities the strategy is called Mutual Assured Destruction. MAD is based on the theory that, if the other side knows that most of his cities and industry may be destroyed in retaliation if he attacks you suddenly (pre-emptively), he won't make the attack in the first place. The other side's cities and civilian population are hostages to your nuclear deterrence.

The level of threat to civilian populations is enormous: world nuclear arsenals are equivalent to 1,250,000 Hiroshima-size bombs – vastly in excess of what is required for deterrence by Mutual Assured Destruction.

But simply reducing this enormous overkill will not solve the problem according to Dr Barnaby, and media focus on arms cuts has been misleading, because danger arises not simply from the number of nuclear weapons, but also from the policies for which they are the means of implementation. Essentially, the established system of defensive retaliation (deterrence) is changing now to one of (offensive) nuclear war-fighting. Instead of the ultimate threat of unleashing a nuclear retaliation in which there would be no winners, new weapons and policies are being introduced designed specifically to facilitate the use of nuclear forces in limited ways to fight and win a nuclear war. This radical shift from deterrence against *any* use to plans-*for*-use has been made possible by technological developments, mainly in the accuracy of delivery systems.

The terrifying conclusion Dr Barnaby reaches is that with current research and development:

... accurate nuclear weapons are, in other words, most likely to change the nuclear policy from nuclear deterrence to nuclear war-fighting. This change is likely to occur whether or not the political leadership wants to make the change. It happens because of technological developments.

Thus, he says, 'preventing qualitative improvements in the nuclear arsenals should be the first priority. Reducing the numbers of nuclear weapons should come afterwards.'

Children and the Nuclear Mentality

This vast subject – touched on in several of the chapters which follow – requires cross-cultural studies in depth of how child-rearing practices may contribute to the nuclear mentality, and of the effects on children of living under the nuclear threat. How do different cultures deal with young children's earliest needs for dependency and containment of their very 'primitive' (psychotic) anxieties? How do they foster a sense of self? What is the major loyalty demanded – is it to the family, religion, nation, or world? Professor Hinde[52] suggests that 'the future lies in perceiving not the nation but humankind as the in-group.'

There are some hopeful signs that this is coming about. A Finnish psychologist, Tytti Solantaus,[88] has found that due to the mass media the global world has become a new developmental domain, a new 'zone of proximal development' and says: 'This domain might be especially relevant in adolescence when one is in the process of establishing one's own identity and one's own way of life.'

However, for this to occur 'new thinking' must predominate in family, school, community, nation and media. It seems that Freud's definition of a healthy adult – one able 'to love and to work' – needs enlarging to include 'and to hold an inclusive world-view'.

In looking at developmental issues one needs also to ask what enables some adults to think for themselves and deal with reality issues while many others project this vital individual responsibility into the ideological groups to which they belong, into the leaders within them, and into technology with all the frightening consequences this has. Several chapters address these questions. Professor Norman Dixon refers elsewhere[21] to the 1981 Carnegie Commission report on US colleges:

Unless we find better ways to educate ourselves as citizens, we run the risk of drifting unwittingly into a new kind of Dark Ages – a time when small cadres of specialists will control knowledge and thus control the decision-making process ... claiming to understand the complex issues and therefore able to tell us what we should believe and how we should act.

One fifth of children under five in the Third World die – from meningitis, anaemia, tetanus, malnutrition, worm infestation and from various diseases which in children in the Western world are prevented by early inoculation. Finance and cooperation by world experts could eliminate these illnesses, as has been achieved with smallpox. But we continue to allow billions of pounds and dollars to be spent creating and deploying more and more death-dealing rather than health-giving equipment. Why?

Dr John Bowlby,[9] the famous British child psychiatrist and psychoanalyst, interviewed on his eightieth birthday said: 'It is in the underdeveloped countries that many infants and young children have the best circumstances for growing up and in the richest that they have the worst.' He explained that Western care-takers have long since learned to take responsibility for a child's physical health, but don't want to take responsibility for its mental health – providing the warm, intimate, continuous relationships that young children need. It is inconvenient, it involves a lot of hard work, and good parenting is not particularly valued – it is not a status-giving occupation in our culture (as Isabel Menzies has also pointed out[68]). But Dr Bowlby warned: 'Deprived children are a source of social infection as real and serious as are carriers of diphtheria and typhoid.'

This raises the question of what links might exist between childhood deprivation and the nuclear mentality, including the need for enemies. 'I am no different from a paediatrician who says your child gets rickets because of lack of vitamin D', concluded Bowlby, prescribing for young children care which deals with their needs for attachment, dependency, emotional expression and learning. If these needs are not met children are unable to develop their capacities for caring and concern for others, thinking and dealing with their feelings and impulses rather than acting them out or inhibiting them with rigid defences, nor respond creatively and responsibly as individuals. If parents cannot meet these needs there must be others who can, and day-care institutions which provide good-quality care with high child/staff ratios.[VI] This prescription, as any other, involves cost. The European Commission's Child Care Network[30] placed child-care provision in Britain as among the worst in quality and lowest in public funding in Europe. By contrast, Britain spends one million pounds per day on nuclear weapons.

Political Thinking, Leadership, Group and Individual Processes

Professor Norman Dixon in Chapter 2, 'Why do leaders mislead?', looks at the factors which can cause leaders to make misguided decisions and the disastrous consequences that can ensue. This is particularly terrifying in situations where decisions have to be made about nuclear matters, as mistakes here lead not to dozens or hundreds but to millions of lives being lost and the destruction of much of the earth as we know it.

One of the many causative factors he describes is that of group-process pressures, together with personality traits and stress. These pressures are also carefully analysed in Chapters 3 and 4 by Anton Obholzer and Hanna Segal. Dr Segal describes how we need groups and the support of others for the positive and constructive part of our natures but how we need them also to contain our maladaptive and more destructive parts. The groups we belong to help over-come individual anxieties, particularly extreme, primitive, psychotic-type anxiety. But, in groups as in individuals, they also provide defence mechanisms which are not always realistic or advantageous. Indeed these group defences if used by individuals would be regarded as psychotic: self-idealisation, grandiosity, omnipotence, paranoia and freedom from conscious guilt (the latter because we merge our superego – or conscience – with the group so that for example, soldiers can kill). But Dr Obholzer shows that we pay a heavy price for our feeling of security in a group and our loyalty to it. Individual doubts and questions are not wanted and the group's denial of reality becomes our own.

Psychological processes in the individual which lead to these maladaptive group-processses are intensified by the nuclear threat under which we live. Dr Segal has said elsewhere[84] that the effect of the nuclear mentality is 'deep terror rooted in the psychotic layers of our unconscious'. She cites Glover[40] in saying that this is because our worst nightmares can now come true, as the boundaries of reality are no longer clearly distinguishable. This terror leads to the use of the psychotic defences which Dr Segal discusses in Chapter 4. She sees the doctrine of nuclear deterrence as based on the state inducing terror in the supposed enemy, but also arousing the same terror to control its own population. The effects on us of the state-induced terror of nuclear weapons are both inner and outer: we both control ourselves (denying and disowning many aspects of our response to the nuclear threat) and we are also controlled externally. As Dr Segal says, 'one has only to consider the gradual erosion of civil liberties in Great Britain in the name of national security.' Secrecy can be used to support the secret-keepers' omnipotence and superiority, especially on issues where truth is needed for people to be able to think and act in a rational way. The British government's secret decision to go ahead with the Chevaline nuclear warhead project in the 1970s is an example of this.

In Chapter 6 Professor John Eldridge wonders where, in such a secretive environment, the press can get access to accurate information from which the public can make informed and rational decisions. He cites the difficulties journalists had during the Falklands war: 'an obsession with security gets in the way of a full flow of information.' He questions what the effect on the press is of operating in a 'deterrence culture', and sees the secrecy and selection of information as allowing the escalation of the arms race.

Dr Segal explains that in a small group its acknowledged 'work-task' can keep psychotic processes at bay, but this is more difficult in a large group and even more so in a state or nation where there is no single, clear work-task to which the group's activity is directed. In states and nations psychotic functions are delegated to subgroups – messianic and grandiose delusions to religious groups; omnipotent power to political groups; killing to the army (and the way military training and ethos are based on paranoid assumptions is described by Alastair Mackie in Chapter 9). In some cases several functions can be found together, for example in fascism, communism, and the fundamentalist movements of Islam and Christianity where the military and messianic functions are combined. As Dr Segal says in Chapter 4 'unthinkingly we adopt the mental posture of the group to which we belong, a posture which may be quite irrational and dangerous for our survival' – for example, the present situation with regard to nuclear weapons policy. Here denial is the main group defence mechanism employed, but other psychotic schizoid defence processes such as projection and depersonalisation are also involved.

Our megalomania, says Segal, can also be aroused by thoughts of global warfare leading to feelings of terror and guilt and the consequent projection of our own destructiveness outside where we can see it only in others, not ourselves. Thus individual and group defence mechanisms often reinforce each other.

Segal asks why, faced with the nuclear threat, we cannot use our sanity? She and Dr Obholzer suggest it is because this sanity, too, can be projected into leaders whom we then idealise (at the same time as denigrating the enemy). 'They'll keep us safe', we say, just as children do with their parents until adolescence when reality impinges and parental feet of clay become apparent. However, in some Western countries reality does not seem to dawn in the case of the nuclear issue: we seem stuck in collective childhood in relation to our leaders. Is this because we have thrown up governments and leaders that express our own defensive processes in order for us not to have to see the real danger, and not to have to take personal responsibility for doing something about it? It is time that we do see the dangers and do take responsibility for our own aggression as well as reclaiming our own capacity for concern and realistic thinking.

Values and Assumptions of Nuclear Weapons Decision-makers

Scilla Elworthy of the Oxford Research Group makes it clear in Chapter 7 how out of touch with reality is the small group of nuclear weapons decision-makers in Britain. She outlines their major assumptions and shows how, even if the political arena is changing, they see no need for their policies to change. She also shows how unaware they are of any non-rational processes and how they assume that leaders are always in control!

Air Commodore Mackie considers the military's inherent resistance to change in Chapter 9. He suggests that one of the factors which brought the Soviet military to acquiesce in change was new circumstances in the Middle East – Islam, Israel, the Gulf War, Libya. This led them to see that area rather than Europe as the main risk area and to change their force dispositions and command structure accordingly.

The West's response to the change in Soviet thinking was to try to cast NATO in a world role, to develop a new maritime strategy and a new land strategy involving the first use of nuclear weapons – 'to seek a problem for every solution'. Mackie identifies the shared characteristics in the British military mind as discipline, uniformity, a devotion to hierarchy, closed minds, and a cleavage to 'my service right or wrong'.

On that basis, he says 'expecting the military to do their duty in a way so radically different from what they currently conceive it to be is a tall order.' But he still has a vision of 'the British military genius emancipated at last, leading NATO towards Common Security and the two alliances out of the Bomb culture'. He calls on the medical profession to bulldoze the military into 'accepting the inescapable logic of strategy and doing something about their doom-laden fixation on the Bomb'.

Edy Korthals Altes describes in Chapter 11 why he resigned his post as Dutch Ambassador to Spain in protest against his country's nuclear policy. He gives powerful reasons why the strategy of MAD (Mutual Assured Destruction) should change to Mutual Assured Security. He outlines a comprehensive approach to international relations which would lead from confrontation towards cooperation. Finally, he reminds us that all our new concepts will come to nothing unless they are supported by a profound change of mind, 'a reorientation of our thinking'. He calls for cooperation among the great religions – together with the humanistic tradition – to provide us with the essential moral and spiritual basis for this reorientation.

Armorer Wason believes that finding practical ways to make it possible for people to change their minds is very important. She has found that direct contact between people from Britain and the USSR has enormous potential, and gives examples of the heartening effects of 'exchanges' on individuals and communities. 'It is the process of working together to solve challenges that cements our relationships', she says, and her experiences offer a positive and practical example of how people can, with courage and hope, break down the nuclear mentality.

We hope that the insights and examples offered in this book will encourage more people to respond creatively to what – despite the misleading media focus on arms cuts – is in 1989 an increasing prospect of nuclear holocaust, as the acknowledged defence expert Dr Frank Barnaby explains in Chapter 1.

Closing the Conference of medical professionals on which this book is based, the President of MCANW Sir Raymond Hoffenberg said: 'We have recently seen strong protest from the medical profession about the threatened dismantling of the health service (in Britain). I should like to see an equally strong protest against the nuclear threat to the future of mankind.'

Part I
The Current Situation

1

The Nuclear Arms Race: Running Hard

FRANK BARNABY

There is a current perception, fed largely by the media, that recent nuclear disarmament initiatives, and possible new ones centred on strategic nuclear weapons, mean that we can all relax about the dangers of nuclear war. This, however, is far from the case.

The nuclear strategies of the USA and USSR are changing dramatically because of technological advances in nuclear weapons and their supporting technologies. The new strategies will considerably increase the risk that nuclear war will occur, either intentionally or by accident. Qualitative advances (so-called modernisation) in nuclear weaponry are, therefore, much more dangerous than mere increases in numbers of nuclear weapons. This is why treaties – like the existing Intermediate Nuclear Forces (INF) Treaty and the Strategic Arms Reduction Treaty (START) now being negotiated – do nothing to reduce the risk of nuclear war, even though they may improve East–West relations. Only measures that would actually stop the nuclear arms race, such as a comprehensive test ban, will now reduce the risk of nuclear war.

NATO's current policy of 'flexible response', for example, is supposedly based on a 'ladder of escalation' starting with the use of low-yield nuclear weapons to counter a Warsaw Pact attack with conventional weapons and then, if necessary, escalating to larger nuclear weapons. The final rung in NATO's ladder of escalation is the use of US strategic nuclear weapons, targeted on Soviet cities and industry.

NATO says that its nuclear strategy is one of nuclear deterrence based on assured destruction. Because the Soviets have similar strategic capabilities the strategy is called Mutual Assured Destruction. MAD is based on the theory that, if the other side knows that most of their cities and industry may be destroyed in retaliation if they attack you suddenly (pre-emptively), they won't make the attack in the first place. The other side's cities and civilian population are hostages to your nuclear deterrence.

A paradox of the nuclear age is that nuclear deterrence based on assured destruction only works with inaccurate nuclear weapons. As more accurate nuclear weapons are deployed the enemy may assume that your nuclear weapons are targeted not on their cities but on their nuclear forces, so destroying their means of retaliation and deterring aggression. The cities then cease to be effective hostages. Accurate nuclear weapons weaken and eventually kill nuclear deterrence based on assured destruction, leading to its opposite – considerations of how and when a nuclear war can be fought and won.

For deterrence based on Mutual Assured Destruction a relatively small number of strategic nuclear weapons is needed – enough to target the enemy's significant cities. In each of the two Super-powers there are at most 200 cities with populations greater than about 100,000 people. Assuming that two nuclear weapons are needed to destroy a large city, about 400 warheads would be more than enough for adequate minimum nuclear deterrence; more than enough, in fact, to kill roughly 100 million people in each Super-power and destroy about half its industrial capability. In spite of this, each Superpower has deployed 10,000 strategic nuclear warheads – 96 per cent of which are overkill. Even if the START Treaty currently being negotiated succeeds in cutting strategic nuclear weapons by 50 per cent, each side will still have about 6,000 nuclear warheads, which is over 90 per cent overkill.

There is no rational strategic reason for having many more than the number of nuclear weapons needed for minimum nuclear deterrence. A much larger nuclear force is likely to lead to a move away from nuclear deterrence based on assured destruction, particularly if accurate nuclear weapons are deployed. In military jargon these are 'counterforce' rather than 'countercity' weapons.

With accurate nuclear weapons, capable of destroying even very hardened military targets, nuclear war-fighting based on the destruction of hostile military forces becomes the preferred policy. Accurate nuclear weapons are, in other words, most likely to change the policy from nuclear deterrence to nuclear war-fighting. This change is likely to occur whether or not the political leadership wants to make the change. It happens because of technological developments.

Nuclear war-fighting policies evolve inevitably from the deployment of accurate strategic and tactical nuclear weapons. If tactical nuclear war-fighting weapons are deployed, they will be integrated into military tactics at relatively low levels of military command. The military will then more easily come to believe that if a war occurs nuclear weapons will be used. Nuclear war becomes fightable. And, of course, the military will believe that if they have to fight a war it is winnable; this contradicts the conclusion that deterrence through Mutual Assured Destruction is meant to lead to: that nuclear war is *un*winnable!

The belief in the fightability and winnability of nuclear war will make such a war and its catastrophic consequences more, not less, likely. The deployment of nuclear war-fighting weapons also leads to perceptions that limited nuclear wars and protracted nuclear wars are possible. These increase the probability that a deliberate nuclear war will occur. Also, the more sophisticated nuclear weapons systems become and the more complex nuclear strategies become, the greater is the danger that nuclear war will break out by miscalculation or accident.

With modern guidance systems nuclear warheads can be delivered over intercontinental distances with great precision – this is the most crucial qualitative advance in nuclear weapons. For example, they can be fitted with a terminal guidance system in which a laser or radar in the nose of the warhead scans the ground around the target as the warhead travels towards it through the Earth's atmosphere. The laser or radar locks onto a distinctive feature in the area, such as a tall building or hill, and guides the warhead with great accuracy to its target.

If current nuclear weapon developments are carried through, all deployed nuclear weapons – tactical and strategic, land-based and sea-based – will soon be nuclear war-fighting weapons. The commonly held view that the very destructiveness of nuclear weapons precludes the outbreak of nuclear war is false and dangerously out of date. Nuclear war is unlikely to occur only if it is believed that neither side can win; this also assumes rational behaviour by politicians and military under great stress. If one power perceives a chance of winning, then there is a risk that it will decide to strike while it has the advantage.

This is particularly likely when one side has a first-strike capability while the other side does not. The Americans are likely to be in such a position of perceived advantage in the late 1990s, as a result of developments taking place now. They will then be under great pressure to use their strategic nuclear advantage before the Soviets acquire the same capability, on the reasoning that international relations would be impossibly unstable if both sides had a first-strike nuclear capability.

Given the risks involved, every effort should be made to prevent the acquisition of a nuclear first-strike capability by negotiating measures to stop and reverse the nuclear arms race. Preventing qualitative improvements in the nuclear arsenals should be the first priority. Reducing the numbers of nuclear weapons should come afterwards.

To make this clear, it may be useful to consider in more detail the current nuclear arsenals and impending developments.

As Table 1.1 shows, of the seven countries possessing nuclear weapons, the Superpowers have the vast majority. Of the other countries we know that Israel has about 150 from the evidence of Mordecai Vanunu, the Israeli technician who gave us this information and was abducted and imprisoned for his pains.

Table 1.1 World Nuclear Arsenals
(approximate number of warheads)

USA	25,000
USSR	25,000
UK	500
France	500
China	300
Israel	150
South Africa	?

Most people believe South Africa has a few nuclear weapons. Additionally, India and Pakistan may be on the verge of a nuclear arms race, with Pakistan about to test a nuclear device. Despite the change in government there, the consensus is that the nuclear weapons programme is continuing.

Nuclear weapons are divided into different categories according to their range – these are diplomatic and legal distinctions, as opposed to technical and military. According to these definitions, 'strategic' nuclear weapons are those with ranges over 5,500 kilometres, whilst those with ranges up to 5,500 kilometres are termed 'tactical'. On that basis, the Superpowers have 12,000 strategic nuclear weapons each, and about 13,000 tactical nuclear weapons each. About 10,000 of these tactical weapons are deployed in Europe. This includes 2,000 which are covered by the recent INF Treaty, which means that when they have been completely removed in two years' time that Treaty will have reduced the nuclear arsenals only by about 4 per cent, leaving 96 per cent in place and, as we shall see, being 'modernised'. Moreover, under the INF Treaty only the launching systems are being destroyed, with the nuclear warheads being recycled for use in new nuclear weapons.

Table 1.2 shows the explosive power of the Superpowers' nuclear arsenals. It is clear that, on the whole, strategic nuclear weapons are more powerful than tactical weapons. The total explosive power in their arsenals is about 15,000 million tonnes of TNT, equivalent to about 1,250,000 Hiroshima-sized bombs. This is an enormous destructive capacity, way beyond any conceivable rational use.

Table 1.2 Explosive Power of US and Soviet Nuclear Forces

	No. of warheads	*Explosive power* (megatons)
USA:		
strategic	13,000	3,500
tactical	11,000	2,500
USSR:		
strategic	11,000	6,000
tactical	15,000	3,000
Total:	50,000	15,000

The INF Treaty complicated considerably the legal distinctions between nuclear weapons, because the diplomats found it necessary to divide tactical weapons into several sub-categories: 'intermediate' defined as ranges from 500 to 5,500 kilometres, and 'short-range' defined as up to 500 kilometres. The intermediate sub-category was itself further divided into 'long-range intermediate' (1,800 to 5,500 kilometres) and 'short-range intermediate' (500 to 1,800 kilometres). The distribution of tactical nuclear weapons between these categories in Europe and the types of weapon are shown in Table 1.3.

Table 1.3 US and Soviet Tactical Nuclear Weapons Deployed in Europe

		Range (km)	No. deployed	No. of warheads
Intermediate nuclear forces – long-range				
USA:	Pershing II*	1,800	108	108
	GLCM*	2,500	208	208
USSR:	SS20*	5,000	441	1,300
	SS4*	2,000	112	112
	short-range			
USSR:	SS12/22*	100	108+	
	SS23*	500	20+	
Short-range nuclear forces				
NATO:	Lance	130		320 on 36 launchers
France:	Pluton	120	44	
USSR:	Frog	70 ⎫	950	
	SS21	120 ⎭		
	Scud	300	7,725	

* to be removed under INF Treaty

The American Cruise (GLCM) and Pershing II and Soviet SS20 and SS4 missiles which fall into the first category are to be removed under the INF Treaty. In addition, the Soviet Union agreed to put into the Treaty their short-range intermediate missiles, the SS12 and SS23. These total approximately 2,000 missiles, leaving still deployed in Europe the short-range missiles which form the second main category in Table 1.3. In the UK NATO has the Lance missile, and there is much controversy currently over the updating of these missiles with greatly increased range. France, in addition to its Pluton, has a new missile under development called Hades, which is due for deployment with a neutron warhead. The Soviet Union has several types of short-range missile: the Frog and Scud are virtually obsolete, while the more modern SS21 has a similar range to NATO's existing Lance. The Soviets say this completes their modernisation programme, which has been underway for some time.

When the INF Treaty has removed these weapons in two years' time there will be in Europe six types of nuclear weapon (Table 1.4). Of these, Pershing IA is bracketed because it was included in the INF Treaty, although, being West German-owned, the USA had no right to bargain it away.

Table 1.4 Nuclear Weapons in Europe Post-INF Treaty (no. of warheads)

	USA	NATO*	TOTAL
Bombs (aircraft)	1,400	300	1,700
Depth charges	150	50	200
Lance (100 launchers)	320	380	700
Artillery: 203 mm	500	400	900
155 mm	600	150	750
(Pershing1A)		(100)	
Sub-total:			4,350
Total (incl. ADMs, naval, SLBMs, British and French):			6,000

*US warheads for use on non-US delivery systems

In addition to those 4,350 nuclear weapons which will remain in Europe after the INF Treaty, there are over 100 atomic demolition munitions (ADMs) – land-mines which were intended in the 1950s for burying along the border but instead are simply stored in Europe. Also, European waters contain several hundred and probably more US naval nuclear weapons assigned to NATO, and submarine-launched ballistic missiles (SLBMs) assigned in a tactical role. Finally, there are about 1,000 British and French nuclear weapons. These various post-INF nuclear weapons total about 6,000 – which is not significantly different from the 7,000 approximately of the late 1950s and early 1960s.

This already bad situation is changing, however, for the worse.

There are several major new US nuclear weapons programmes under way (Table 1.5). The MX missile was first deployed in fixed silos in 1986 and remains an issue because the original intention of making it mobile is still being considered. There are particular difficulties and hazards with mobile basing of nuclear missiles. There are 50 MX missiles each with ten warheads.

Table 1.5 Major New US Strategic Nuclear Weapons Programmes

	Year of deployment	*Number*
MX	1986	50 each with 10 warheads*
Trident II	1989	? US + ? UK
B-1B bomber	1986	100
Advanced Cruise	1989	?
Midgetman	1992	500 planned, each with 1 warhead

* deployed currently; 50 more may be deployed

Trident II being deployed now is specially noteworthy because it is the first submarine-launched ballistic missile to be as accurate as land-based missiles and able to destroy the other side's retaliatory weapons. This makes it a dangerously destabilising weapon, and certainly not a deterrent. Until Trident, SLBMs were not sufficiently accurate to hit Soviet strategic forces and command centres. They were targeted on Soviet cities. So until recently there was the strange situation of the US Air Force and Soviet rocket forces with extremely accurate weapons operating non-deterrent war-fighting policies, whereas the two navies with less accurate weapons targeted each other's cities operating deterrence by Mutual Assured Destruction! The two policies are quite different, with different constraints, risks and consequences. As a result of Trident II, US and NATO nuclear navies are now changing from deterrence via MAD to join their air- and land-based forces in a comprehensive nuclear war-fighting policy.

When Mrs Thatcher supports 'our deterrent forces', therefore, she is talking about a policy which no longer operates as a result of prolonged and extremely costly technological developments. This makes her frequent assertions about deterrence extremely misleading.

The USAF B1-B bomber, flown by computer, uses new Stealth technology to avoid detection. When it is through its current development problems – there have been several expensive crashes recently – about 100 of them will be deployed. The Advanced Cruise missile follows the terrain to evade radar detection like the existing Cruise to be removed from Greenham Common under the

INF Treaty, but it is supersonic and will reach Eastern Europe much more quickly.

Newest of the American strategic developments is the Midgetman, a mobile single-warhead missile of which 500 are planned. Whether MX will be made mobile, and instead of or as well as Midgetman, is still undecided in Washington. Together they will add 1,000 mobile strategic warheads of great accuracy to the existing, swollen nuclear arsenals. (President Reagan typically confused matters by offering, in an apparently impromptu way, to put US mobile missiles into the current START talks. But since then many in the Pentagon and Bush administration have strongly resisted this.)

It is in the great accuracy and reduced flight-times of these new American strategic weapons that the new dangers lie. They depart from the old concept of deterrence through Mutual Assured Destruction to provide instead the capacity for a pre-emptive first-strike. Simply the perception of this capability is destabilising.

New supporting technologies are an integral part of these US nuclear war-fighting developments, including anti-submarine warfare, SDI (Star-Wars) and anti-satellite technologies. These are very much part of the new arms race. The combination of these supporting technologies with the new war-fighting weapons already described will undoubtedly give the USA a first-strike capability. However much politicians deny this, technologically and militarily it is a fact. The question is how, politically, will this new capability operate? Will it make nuclear war extremely likely and virtually inevitable? Personally, I think it will.

In developing such technologies, the USSR is three to five years behind the USA. Currently it has deployed two mobile intercontinental ballistic missile systems (SS24, SS25), while a long-range SLBM (SS-NX-23) which may later approach Trident's capacity is being developed. The Blackjack bomber is similar to but less advanced than the American B1-B. Finally, there is a new Soviet air-launched Cruise missile, the AS-15.

Tactical as well as strategic nuclear forces are being changed from deterrence to a war-fighting capability. This is being achieved by 'modernising' nuclear artillery, by extending the range of Lance (and possibly putting it in the Mobile Launcher Rocket System which also takes conventional missiles, creating great verification problems for the future), and by a new air-to-surface nuclear missile. This latter (SRAM) is planned for 1995, with a short-range tactical variant (SRAM-T). A British version of this is also planned, with at least a British warhead to keep the Aldermaston Atomic

Weapons Establishment busy once it has finished with Trident.

Comparing the sum of these developments with the immediate post-INF nuclear arsenals shows little difference in absolute numbers, and serious differences in security implications. In 1995 one can foresee that nuclear bombs on aircraft will be reduced to about 700, with 200 naval depth charges, 1,000 air-to-surface and 800 surface-to-surface missiles, 600 nuclear artillery shells, 400 submarine-launched Cruise missiles and 1,000 British and French missiles, totalling approximately 5,000 nuclear warheads in Europe in 1995. This means that talk in NATO of considerable reductions is very misleading. And when you take into account the war-fighting as opposed to deterrent capacity of these new strategic and tactical nuclear weapons, and the near-total reliance on complex computerised decision-making systems, the foreseeable future is highly alarming. These concerns about the immediate nuclear future are itemised in Table 1.6.

Table 1.6 Nuclear Concerns

Technological developments
    Very accurate missiles
    Very short flight-times
    Mobile basing modes
    Complex vulnerable command/control/communications

Consequences:
    Nuclear war-fighting policy replaces deterrence via MAD
    Computerised decision-making and launch-on-warning
    procedures

Future technological developments
    Effective anti-submarine warfare systems
    Effective anti-ballistic missile systems (e.g. SDI)
    Effective anti-satellite warfare systems

Consequences:
    Nuclear war-fighting becomes nuclear war-winning (i.e. first-
    strike) policy

Note

Data in Tables are from current publications of the Stockholm International Peace Research Institute and of the International Institute for Strategic Studies.

Part II
Causes and Consequences

2

Why Do Leaders Mislead?

NORMAN DIXON

Leaders are popularly regarded as people who, by direction and encouragement, help others to achieve group goals. Without them social cooperation and therefore civilisation would be difficult, if not impossible.

But there is a grimmer side to leadership. Between Attila the Hun and the present day, dubious decisions by military and political leaders have cost many hundreds of millions of human lives. Losses sustained by followers may be relatively slight or excessively large. Whereas Idi Amin, once described by his British commanding officer as 'a great chap to have around', contented himself with killing a mere 500,000 of his fellow Ugandans, Pol Pot felt constrained to murder three million Kampucheans. To date pride of place must go to Stalin who in 30 years rid himself of some 30 million people who, for one reason or another, were getting in the way.

Disagreeable though these tyrants have been, their behaviour did not threaten anything approaching the total extinction of the species.

However, the destructive forces which in recent years technology has put at the disposal of world leaders do threaten to destroy humanity and should prompt us to question what leaders do and why they do it.

Top-level leadership today may be characterised in terms of a basically incompatible relationship – that between something warm, soft, slow, wet, sentient and unreliable and something cold, hard, fast, devoid of feelings but infinitely destructive. In other words, fallible human beings on the one hand and weapons of mass destruction on the other. Allowing the former to control the latter is on a par with giving Little Miss Muffet a chainsaw to deal with her spider problem.

In case this seems unfair, consider these recent mishaps at the man/machine interface: the world's worst aircraft accident resulted from the incorrigible behaviour of two highly experienced pilots at

Tenerife which wiped out 582 of their 'followers' – this happened even before their planes were off the ground; consider also the loss within a matter of days of two Airbuses, one through the over-riding of its technological aids, the other through over-reliance on modern technology; three major catastrophes at nuclear power stations, in Britain, the USA and USSR; a succession of major railway accidents; and very recently the world's most devastating oil slick which, typically, none of those involved believed could happen. Add to this the thousands who die every year on the roads and one cannot escape the conclusion that, when in charge of technology with the potential for releasing immensely destructive forces, mankind is hardly to be trusted. All of this suggests we would do well to look closely at those political or military leaders who are responsible for administering the ultimate in lethal tech-nology: nuclear weaponry. How, why, and in what ways are they likely to mislead?

There are, in fact, three ways: by self-deception as to what they are about, by deceiving their followers as to the realities of a situa-tion, and by making such inept decisions that their followers are literally led astray.

While the three forms of misleading are not mutually exclusive the first two are most usually the special province of politicians, and the last that of their executives – military leaders.[20,21]

Political leaders favour deception for a variety of fairly obvious reasons. Lying and empty promises are amongst the easiest ways of achieving and, in the short term as exemplified by Nixon, holding on to power. Being economical with the truth is the shortest cut to getting your own way without arousing criticism or opposition to your wishes. The preservation of secrecy (a form of passive lying) confers a sense of power and is therefore both a substantial ego-boost for the tight-lipped guardians of information and an effective smokescreen for bumbling incompetence.

As for self-deception – without the benefit of this anodynal defence mechanism even such appalling creatures as the erstwhile rulers of Haiti and of the Philippines might have been deterred by doubts about their actions or what would eventually happen to them.

No less serious than deliberate or even unconscious deception, indeed their main spur, are the hazards which attend executive decisions.

When considering the reasons why leaders lead people astray, pride of place must surely be given to those personality factors which, through self-selection, characterise the big mis-leaders. The argument is simple, if not banal. People are attracted to and prosper in vocations which suit their mental make-up. As a consequence it is not surprising to find amongst the ranks of political leaders some who are power-hungry, manipulative, extrovert, sensation-seeking, theatrical, exhibitionistic, devious, pragmatic, prepared to take risks, and certainly not weighed down with moral scruples. For good or bad the natural characteristics of such people, encouraged by the job they are trying to do, will determine the decisions they make.

Amongst military leaders, on the other hand, we may expect to find a very different personality-type: people who are authoritarian, rule-bound, conforming, obedient, honourable, but unimaginative.

Of course there have been and no doubt still are many wondrous exceptions to these rules of thumb – noble statespeople steeped in self-denying altruism and brilliantly innovative generals. But we are concerned with the worst scenario – the bad luck (for the world) case of an obedient closed-minded military executive implementing the decisions of a maverick politician. In this nuclear age such a union could spell complete and permanent quietude for millions of their followers.

An additional problem for both sorts of decision-maker, political and military, is that of incomplete or ambiguous information. Faced with the fact that we rarely, if ever, have sufficient information on which to make such momentous decisions as who to marry or whether or not to unleash a nuclear war, it is hardly encouraging to learn that, by and large, human beings seem 'wired' for optimism.

Through denial of the unpalatable, misinterpretation, distortion or repression of the unacceptable, and a predeliction for wish-fulfilling fantasies, decisions tend to be based not on what is the case but on what we would like to be the case.

When a need for peace of mind takes precedence over that for survival the anticipated outcomes of a decision may well seem rosier than they deserve. Add to this the fact that the more emotionally important and the less warranted a decision the greater will be attempts to justify it and we have all the ingredients for such fiascos as Eden's Suez, Kennedy's Bay of Pigs, and Operation Market Garden (the Arnhem adventure in the Second World War).

Optimal decisions, choosing the best of possible options, depend on motives that are relevant to the desired goal. So when leaders are swayed by such egocentric desires as their need to be liked, the urge to strike a macho image, to boost self-esteem, to appear young and spritely, to distract attention from their shortcomings or to emulate some great leader of the past, the chances are that their decisions will be biased away from what is best for their followers. Since these motives are often synonymous with those which get such people to positions of power in the first place, they tend to be the stock-in-trade of leaders who mislead.

It is more than likely that such life or death decisions as whether or not to launch nuclear missiles at the enemy will be made during a period of intense stress for the decision-maker. Faced with an awesome choice it is highly likely that the decision-maker will be handicapped both physically and mentally by that biological anachronism, the adrenergic 'fight or flight' emergency response. This reaction, ideally suited to those physical threats which can be countered by the rapid expenditure of muscular energy – such as striking or running away from an attacker – is singularly inappropriate to the complex cognitive problems facing high-level decision-makers today. Having evolved over millions of years to cope with and survive in a habitat which is radically different from the present one, our brains simply don't work in the sort of ways that allow us to interact successfully or safely with modern technology.

Such concomitants of stress as narrowed attention, perceptual distortion, impaired memory, slowed thinking, not to mention physical disorders ranging in severity from indigestion and headache to cardiac arrest, are just some of the symptoms which could afflict even the most dedicated leaders. And this at the very time when they should be giving of their best!

So unpleasant are the effects of stress that the sufferers might well resort to alcohol or other drugs to make themselves feel better. But, as typified by the performances of many leaders,[58] including Eden during the Suez crisis and Hitler in the Second World War, medication for stress is often counterproductive. When blurred by alcohol or hyped up with amphetamines the tendency to mislead is likely to become more rather than less pronounced.

A further point concerns the role of possessing lethal technology in the decision-making of leaders who could launch a nuclear attack. Hopefully the knowledge that they have the wherewithal to exterminate humanity might make them adopt a less aggressive stance. But the evidence suggests that the possession of weapons would probably have quite the opposite effect. According to several researchers[7] the presence (let alone ownership) of a gun makes people behave more rather than less belligerently. A weapon is, it seems, a stimulus to violence. If the mere sight of a gun can bias decisions towards aggressive options, what of this so-called weapons-effect when a leader knows that he or she possesses an arsenal of nuclear weapons?

The weapons-effect demonstrates, it has been said, that 'the trigger pulls the finger'. So what of the political leader, already stressed, whose trigger is a telephone connected to Air Force Strike Command or a Trident submarine?

So much for some of the more obvious reasons why leaders mislead. There are others, of a more malignant and intractable kind, such as because leaders are excessively paranoid or psychopathic, because they are grandiose and corrupted by enjoying too much power for too long, because they are driven by and acting out infantile complexes, or because they are trying to compensate for feelings of inferiority sown early in childhood. A particular problem for intensely paranoid leaders is that any information or event which threatens to contradict their most cherished beliefs may actually intensify rather than reduce their persecutory delusions. Deeply suspicious of the apparently contradictory evidence and incapable of ever admitting they might have been wrong, leaders of this ilk become even more prone to initiating some dangerous action which seems, to them, justified as self-protective or retaliatory.

The foregoing sources of error are summarised in Figure 2.1. Not only do they interact with each other, magnifying the likelihood of wrong decisions, but the stressful consequences of an initial misjudgement can set off a whole chain of further errors. And the worst thing about leaders who mislead is that being inordinately self-protective and deeply bunkered they will probably outlast the rest of us.

Figure 2.1 Why Leaders Mislead: Sources of Error

Information	*Needs*	*Stress*
Insufficient	Irrelevant & disruptive	Anxiety, fear & anger
	– for approval	Uncertainty
Inaccurate	self-esteem	Responsibility
	macho image	Boredom
	conformity	Group pressures
Ambiguous	achievement	Social isolation
False	peace of mind	Overload/scarcity of information
		Sleep loss
		Insomnia
		Alcohol
		Physical & psychological disorders

DECISION-MAKING PROCESS

Personality Traits
Obstinacy
Impulsiveness
Psychopathy
  paranoia
  etc.

3

The Comfort of Groups

A Psychoanalytic Perspective on Group and Institutional Processes

ANTON OBHOLZER

I find it a cause of constant amazement that society behaves as if individuals and their social institutions run on rational, understandable, conscious lines – amazing because wherever you look the evidence is to the contrary. Decisions are made on arbitrary and illogical criteria, the obvious is denied and an 'ostrich attitude' reigns supreme.

Why should this be? I believe this is an area in which psychoanalysts can make a major contribution because they approach the subject with different assumptions, namely that the everyday behaviour of individuals (and consequently social institutions) is heavily influenced by unconscious processes. The so-called 'logic' of everyday conscious behaviour is nothing but a badly applied veneer on the carcass of unconscious individual and group assumptions.

A System of Defence Against Anxiety

So what are these underlying individual and group assumptions, and why is it necessary to apply a veneer to them? The purpose of the veneer is to make it appear as if we manage ourselves and our social structures in a rational, conscious, controlled way. It is to give the appearance of knowing, of understanding, of being in control, of being master of our fate. It follows that the unconscious fears are of a different and opposite state of mind: of not knowing, of being lost, boundary-less, out of control, at the mercy of hostile forces.

The findings of psychoanalysts confirm this view. Starting with observations on very young children and following the human development cycle it is clear that the earliest relationships have as their task the containing of the child's anxiety and the fostering of a sense of self: the development of a psychological 'skin'. In the earliest stages this serves both as a physical boundary for a sense of self and also as a psychological one. Thus a sense of self, of belonging to a family, a group, an institution, a nation, are all

31

various layers of skin to foster a sense of identity, security and belonging.

They are ways of avoiding being lost in space, boundary-less, unconnected, psychotic. All of these manifestations and anxieties can be regularly observed in clinical work with children and in psychoanalytic work with individuals of all ages. Psychoanalysis describes them as ways of keeping psychotic anxiety at bay. Schools of thought and social structures are thus man-made devices to protect ourselves from these anxieties. Put another way, they are social structures which we join at birth, renewing or not (as the case may be) our membership as we go through life in order to have protection and rescue from isolation and breakdown – a sort of unconscious symbolic vehicle rescue service!

On Belonging to Defensive Systems

But, as with those vehicle rescue services, there is a membership price to pay. The price to pay for membership of these mental and social structures is not to question their functioning but to go along with the system in an unthinking, loyal sort of way.

These structures then do the denial on our behalf – it is as if the contract is along the lines of 'don't worry your head about uncertainties, anxieties, fear of death, annihilation, extinction, etc. – join us and in return for your allegiance we will provide you with a ready-made system of denial and defence – leave it all to us. All we want from you is unquestioned allegiance to our way of doing things.' Personal thought and questioning therefore invalidate membership and return the anxiety to us for us to deal with individually. The essence of these systems of thought and social institution is that they will practise denial on our behalf. In other words, that they will act as mental cooperatives for our own defensive structures – a mass-produced veneer of denial is somehow more credible than a home-produced individual one. After all, others doing it lends a supposed credibility to the process.

It is along the lines of 'if we all pretend that it isn't there, then it isn't there' – a variant of the Emperor's clothes.

The Functioning of Social Systems Against Anxiety

These 'mental defensive cooperatives' take the form of ideologies, schools of thought of political organisations, and beliefs of nationalism, etc. What they all have in common is that they will act defensively on our behalf, to keep the unspeakable and unthinkable at bay.

In doing so they apply the same mechanisms described by psychoanalysts in individual defensive mental functioning, for example as in the patient or family who denies having cancer and behaves as if there were no problem at all. The difficulty with this approach is, of course, that no remedial action can be taken without an inordinate mess resulting. The same process of denial happens on a global basis particularly on nuclear, environmental and chemical warfare issues with the same consequences as in the case of individuals: if the problem is denied then no work can be done in order to ameliorate it.

The mechanism described in the Bible of not seeing the beam in one's own eye but instead seeing the mote in the others is as relevant today as it has ever been. The purpose of mental defensive mechanisms, whether in the individual or in social configurations, is to protect oneself from pain and inner conflict. The traditional way of doing this is by what psychoanalysts call splitting and projective identification. This refers to a process of disowning the usually negative aspects of oneself and seeing them with convincing clarity in the others – a device of projecting the disowned aspects of the self and then identifying them in the other. This device, familiar to all of us, happens not only in individuals but also amongst groups, institutions and nations. And the greater the anxiety at the time, the more prevalent the mechanism and the greater the pseudo-clarity of insight and the resulting self-righteousness.

Thus at times of international crisis it is always the enemy that is warmongering, bloodthirsty, threatening nuclear aggression etc., and it is always oneself who is a righteous defender of the truth.

These mechanisms help to comfort us both as individuals and as members of these defensive cooperatives. The price we pay, however, is that no progress towards resolution of the crisis can be achieved because it is always 'the other side' which is responsible and which, therefore, has to make the first move. It is only through recognition of one's own equal contribution to the problem that movement towards resolution can be made. And thinking about these issues, even the act of reading this book, can be one form of us owning our own contributions to this process.

Membership of these social defensive systems, whilst comforting in the short-term, is in the long-term a most dangerous activity, because it leads to inevitable escalation of the conflict and to a pushing of individual, group and national conflict further and further away, with less and less chance of resolution. It is only through the acceptance of individual and group responsibility that the problem can be acknowledged and worked upon. This applies whether we are talking about personal 'atom bombs in the mind' or the international threat of nuclear warfare.

Defensive Structure and Organisation

There are other aspects of organisational structure that add to their defensive nature. These relate to the use of time and hierarchy in order to diminish personal identity and thus initiative. In most organisations an overall institutional timetable is imposed on members, transforming them from individuals into members of the organisation and in the process tilting them into a more institutionally compliant state of mind. They are then more likely to go along with institutional values and with institutionally-determined defensive patterns.

A timetable imposed as a grid upon the organisation and its members therefore has the function of providing them with a skin of sorts, at the price already mentioned.

Hierarchy and authority in human social structures provide a similar function, and nowhere more so than in the military establishment. The whole induction process into the army – including the stripping of the individual of his personal clothes and possessions and the substitution of identical clothing and equipment – is a concerted attempt to rid him of his identity and turn him from an individual with a name into an organisational substructure with only a number as identity.

This process obviously makes it much easier to 'manage' the individual – a process whereby individual thought and initiative is leached out and corporate identity and allegiance are stressed.

Another standard psychological device is the projection downwards of incompetence. Thus any decision of importance needs to be taken by higher authorities who supposedly know better, and what decisions could be more important than decisions about nuclear warfare?

The psychological state of mind in members of the hierarchy is thus one of 'we don't need to worry about this – they higher up know about it and will make the appropriate decision.' This is a further manifestation of the splitting and projective identification process. Of course it takes no account of what we all know and is daily exposed in the media – the gross incompetence manifest in the highest circles of management. There is no earthly reason to believe that invocations that 'they up there know better' on 'security matters' are generally anything but a defensive cover-up masquerading as something else.

This kind of organisational structure can be presented as being task-orientated – structured in such a way that effective work can be carried out with an effective command. This is true. But it is equally true to say that it is a structure which ensures that the least possible amount of thinking and questioning takes place and therefore that it is the most conservative and resistant of organisations. So this dynamic goes hand in hand with the defensive processes already mentioned, and serves them.

Group and Institutional Factors

Group and institutional factors also play a part in undermining the individual's capacity to think and act upon personal authority.

Psychoanalysts who work at applying psychoanalytic concepts in groups and organisations, as well as social scientists and anthropologists, have long known that there are specific processes arising within groups of various sizes. Thus very small groups recreate aspects of family dynamics.

Small groups numbering up to about 14 or 15 enable members to know and identify each other and to act accordingly. Beyond that point, particularly in the absence of a clear task and structure, it becomes increasingly difficult and the move is towards a faceless mob. It is inevitable that the individual loses his or her identity and becomes a member of the mob being swept along by the group mentality. If the group itself has no clear task and leadership is spontaneous then the group and thus the individual is at the mercy of the most primitive anxieties and defences.

If there is no clear task but leadership is present the group is at the mercy of the sort of processes described so graphically in the Apocrypha in the story of Judith and Holophernes. Holophernes had a much larger army than the besieged Israelites and was obviously a charismatic, autocratic leader. The entire army was identified with him as figurehead. Personal identity was therefore denied and all competence and power projected into him. Judith, by cutting off his head and publicly displaying it, immediately caused the whole system to collapse and the army to disperse.

This was a system where all personal thought was foregone in the service of a cult-figure. This process continues in present-day life and can be read about daily in the press.

The Nuremberg rallies in pre-war Germany, with their pomp and organisation, are another example of a crowd being manipulated, and making itself available to be manipulated, in such a way as to be mindless and entirely under the control of one individual. The individuals that spring up to perform these group leadership functions have a specific individual and group valency. Unstructured large group processes are of such a nature that it is virtually impossible for the individual to resist them. Being an individual in such a group is so lonely as to be very frightening. There is fear that one's very existence is at stake. The pressure on the individual is thus to join the group and to partake in the group mentality, which is such that individual thought, competence and authority are lost and the individual becomes a tool of the group.

The process of group formation and this type of group functioning is more likely to happen in a climate of uncertainty and tension. In turn, this sort of group behaviour further fans the flames of these irrational and psychotic group and individual mechanisms.

Most importantly for us today, it is not necessary for enrolment in these group processes that the group must be actually physically present, though no doubt that gives it added impetus. It is sufficient to be caught up mentally or imaginatively in such a large group process. The news-media function today to co-opt us into membership of large groups, so building a body of opinion about some subject.

Thus it is possible to become a member of a mindless large group by identification with it and by means of media coverage and hype. This is recognised by those who wish to manipulate and influence the public state of mind. It is no coincidence that in a coup the first places the military head for are the radio and television stations.

This process of large group formation, of mindlessness, and of leadership that has as its unconscious task the acting out of the psychotic elements of the group, is not confined to any one side in a conflict. It happens on both sides of a divide. We have not only within-group processes but also between-group processes. Put into a world perspective, therefore, we have a system in which nations act as defensive cooperatives for their own citizens and contract at an unconscious group level to deny personal and national responsibility, instead projecting all negatives into the other side, in this instance the other nation.

Implications for Action

These psychoanalytic insights and their application to individual, group and national settings also have, as an integral part of the process, mechanisms for addressing the problems and working towards their resolution.

A problem cannot be addressed until it is acknowledged, and preferably defined in clear terms. Therefore it is essential that all of us in both our personal and organisational roles constantly work at keeping the nuclear threat foremost in our minds and the public mind. It is in the nature of our personal and social defence mechanisms that denial will constantly encroach on awareness of the dangers of the nuclear threat. The best way of strengthening our resolve is by supporting each other in both structured small groups and in organisations with a clear brief. Hence the importance of organisations such as the Medical Campaign Against Nuclear Weapons, and its conferences and publications.

We should also remember that these social and psychological mechanisms apply to all human and social settings, and that we are no exception to the functioning of these defence mechanisms.

In addressing the problem of splitting and projective identification it is essential to meet with and have ongoing dialogue with 'the other side'. It is only by such contact that we come to the realisation that 'they' are very much like 'us', and that the perception of 'them' as being different, threatening, etc., is a consequence of our denying these qualities in ourselves and perceiving them only in the other side by this process of projective identification.

These projective processes thrive in an uncritical, obedient atmosphere and an overly cohering group. Ongoing dialogue encouraging the expression of differences of opinion in an atmosphere of openness is, therefore, the best way forward on the path to resolution.

There are risks in this process, however, both to us and the resolution of national differences, concerning the general issue of diminishing the nuclear threat.

The risk is that we will fall into a state of mind of believing that our simply being aware of the true state of affairs is enough, forgetting – because it is so difficult – the nature of general recruitment. By that I mean the difficulty of recruiting people away from a comfortable state of mind of denial into an uncomfortable state of awareness with the attendant difficulties of not knowing how to act upon this.

The second risk is that the peace movement itself becomes part of the establishment process, so that organisations such as MCANW become one end of an institutionalised polarity, each pole sustaining the other by its opposition but unable to find the common ground of resolution. The risk is that we become part of some ritualised, stylised debate with the rest of the population withdrawn from the issue – an opposition which is static rather than moving towards resolution, and which closely mirrors the unproductive Superpower confrontation which we say we wish to change. This in itself would be part of a societal defensive process, with the debate delegated to these two constituent elements of society while everybody else is left to get on with their lives as if there were no nuclear threat, or perhaps to get on with denying the threat of death.

This process is also repeated within each side of the debate over nuclear weapons, with anti-nuclear groups and pro-nuclear groups each having their own 'hawks' and 'doves', and in this form can be similarly distracting from the achievement of the groups' declared purposes.

Finally, an issue which arises from the application of psychoanalytic processes to matters of organisation and authority: where does one derive one's authority from in order to proceed in the ways outlined above?

It is a common assumption that authority is derived from some external structure – and if this has not happened yet then it is merely a matter of timing, the 'authority' will somehow be delegated at a later time by some as yet unspecified process. I view this as a form of succumbing to defensive mechanisms, in particular denial. There is no evidence that I am aware of that such authority to act is ever delegated by an external resource.

The authority to act in the service of what one believes to be true is derived solely from within oneself and has to be maintained under pressure of critical group processes. Most of these group pressures arise from the 'group in the mind'. In my view this is the most intimidating of all groups. It is only by acting courageously in the face of these pressures that we can begin as individuals to face some of the horrors before us – in this instance the horror of nuclear warfare. As well as addressing this as individuals we can also team up with other like-minded individuals and, by collectively addressing these issues and by finding together the courage to act, form groups and organisations with a real potential to effect change.

DISCUSSION
Question: Do you think that one's psychological resilience is nourished by receiving more information? It has that effect for me.
Dr Obholzer: Clearly information can both empower and disem-

power. In the work of the Oxford Research Group (Chapter 7) I sense that discovery of information about the nuclear decision-makers has been very empowering. But information, especially if it is painful and presents you with no apparently appropriate response, can also make you feel insignificant, inadequate, so that you feel you have to leave it to others. That is exactly the passive dependency that occurs so often in groups. Perhaps anti-nuclear groups are particularly prone to this because of both the information they focus on and the nature of the groups.

How the group affects you depends on whether it is structured or unstructured, or perhaps I should say relatively and apparently unstructured. Groups which are unstructured like a mob, or the group formed in the mind through the medium of television, are the most destructive of one's independence and integrity; here, individuals give up their ability to think freely and critically and their authority to take independent action based on that. But even in a well-structured group such as the MCANW Conference, with its time-table, formal seating, formal roles of chairperson, speakers, audience (which can only contribute at specified times), we risk falling into a pattern of reliance on the group and losing the motivation of our individual anger. Then, when we're alone later, we feel inadequate in the face of the information we have admitted and taken responsibility for, and feel unsupported, and tend to become passive again.

Scilla Elworthy: Before I could feel confident of interviewing these powerful, secretive men [as part of the Oxford Research Group's study of nuclear decision-makers] I needed information, and the confidence it brings. Even painful information can make you feel stronger – you have more of the truth.

Anger has been a great motivator for me. I remember visiting the UN Special Session on Disarmament in 1982, when nearly one million people gathered in New York's Central Park and petitioned their demands for nuclear disarmament. That was a huge demonstration, you couldn't help but be impressed by the power of the emotions expressed. But next day when I went into the Special Session again it carried on as if nothing had happened, nothing changed, the same worthy speeches about disarmament, and I felt outraged. That made me think that to change anything you have to discover who are the people making these decisions and understand why they make them. We have a great deal of information on the nuclear situation now. Doctors should be able to absorb this and channel it into action and – as professionals – take it straight to the decision-makers themselves.

Dr Obholzer: It is possible, of course, to be both an authority-figure within an hierarchically organised sector of society like medicine, and also in the reverse position in relation to authority in wider society. That is why doctors' remarkable stand against the currently proposed changes in the National Health System in Britain is so encouraging. It seems the medical profession is being shaken out of its passive dependent role in relation to political authority, and taking personal authority for health in a much wider context including the nuclear arena which has, until now, been perceived as a political preserve.

Question: In Holland we wonder why Mrs Thatcher is elected again and again? Many people in Britain don't agree with her or like her. Could it be because she seems so terribly sure of herself, and that gives a false sense of security?

Dr Obholzer: I think the principles I described earlier apply. A great deal of human behaviour individually and institutionally is about trying to avoid personal pain and dilemma. This can be done by finding some orthodoxy to go along with. It is very reassuring to that defensive part of us when someone says, in effect, 'don't worry. I'll take care of it.' One of the hallmarks of Mrs Thatcher's leadership is that there's no doubt, only absolute certainty. We respond in a complicated way: we allow such leadership whilst at the same time disowning it. We disagree with her and feel ourselves to be better people for that but instead of being prompted to reclaim our authority we simply feel absolved of any responsibility or guilt. One might think of an adolescent grumbling about his parents but secretly content to have someone to blame, and despising the comforts of their home which he continues to enjoy.

4

Political Thinking:
Psychoanalytical Perspectives

HANNA SEGAL

We are social animals. As infants we experience our dependence on the maternal breast or its equivalent; gradually we become aware that we depend on our parents, then on the family as a whole. Gradually the group extends to friends, schools, etc. We all belong to a group, and mostly to several groups, such as family, workplace, nation, political allegiance, etc. These groups play an important role in our lives; our thinking is conditioned not only by our individual psychological processes, but also by the nature of group functioning. As adults we need the support of others for our good and constructive parts. But we also need groups to contain the more destructive and sicker parts of our personality.

Freud has said that we form groups for two reasons: to combat the forces of nature, and to control our aggression towards each other. We need groups for external reality reasons, for cooperation to achieve our tasks. But we also need groups for very deep psychological reasons. We seek the security of the group to defend us against anxieties, like a child in the dark needing company. The group helps overcome anxieties, partly in a constructive way, by reinforcing our loving, positive, constructive, realistic parts. But also, as with individual development, groups protect us by defence mechanisms which are not always realistic or for the realistic good of the individual or the group.

Dr Obholzer describes, in the preceding chapter, the price we pay for the security the group gives us. Group defence mechanisms are mainly directed against psychotic anxieties which the individual cannot contain; this is so because these anxieties are the hardest to deal with on our own. These mechanisms, for example self-idealisation, grandiosity and paranoia, if used by an individual, would be considered psychotic. Some French have no doubt that they are the most cultured nation in the world; many British consider theirs the only just and fair society. There was a myth that Poland is the Christ of nations. In normal circumstances, however, the constructive and realistic functions predominate and such

41

psychotic features are kept under control.

Groups are also free of conscious guilt. As Freud has noted, we merge our superegos into a group superego and get rid of individual responsibility and guilt. Soldiers who in their private lives could not bear the guilt of killing carry out genocide without guilt when it is sanctioned by the group or by the authorities.

Wilfred Bion, a British psychoanalyst, extended Freud's hypothesis about the two functions of the group.[8] One he called the work-group, which is the group function of realistic joint work, what Freud would have called combatting the forces of nature. The other he called the basic-assumption group, by which he meant that the other function of the group is handling psychotic anxieties. A basic assumption, as he calls it, is a psychotic premise on which the group functions. Such psychotic premises underlie, for instance, our sense of superiority to other groups, our unwarranted hostility or fear of them. Our individual psychotic parts are merged into our group identity, and we don't feel mad because the group sanctions it. If the work function predominates in the group this is kept in check, and crazy assumptions may be made to seem fairly innocuous.

A large group such as a state or nation can also delegate psychotic functions to subgroups, such as the army, which are kept under control by the group as a whole. The military mind and military training are based on paranoid assumptions. Our sense of dependence on omnipotence and our messianic, grandiose delusions can be vested in churches or religion in general. Other subgroups of the same kind can be formed.

But what happens if the tail starts wagging the dog and the military mentality takes over, and the realistic self-interest of the group, like a nation, becomes subjected to the megalomania and paranoia of war-lords? What happens when the religious subgroup takes over, as in religious wars and inquisitions? Clemenceau it was, I think, who said that war is too important to be left to the generals. At the moment we have two glaring examples, the religious leadership in Iran and the fundamentalist Christians in America who pray for an atomic war to bring Armageddon and save the just. In this case the messianic mentality joins hands with the military mentality.

Similarly, a political grouping such as fascism or communism can combine the army mentality with the religious mentality, bringing about guiltless destruction. The same can happen when the group called the nation becomes ruled by nationalism. Members of a group are brought together because they share common interests and common anxieties. Members of a group brought together by work of whatever kind have a common individual and group interest. The security of both individuals and their groups is bound up with the success of the work. Rivalries are unavoidable but tempered by the need for the group's survival and success – in the same way that the child's security depends on the whole family's welfare despite its jealousies and envies. The group itself can face rivalry with other groups and this too can take a sane form (for instance, a willingness to do as well as or better than another group); or it can take an insane, destructive form liable to destroy both parties.

Political groupings likewise are brought together by common needs and interests. At its simplest, the rich man or the oppressor, unable to face guilt about his destructiveness or ambition, joins others in denying the guilt in two ways: one is the creation of a joint group superego and the other is the projection of destructiveness and guilt into the poor and oppressed. The poor, on the other hand, feel helpless, vengeful and envious; they too deal in projection and self-idealisation.

The predominance of the psychotic function over the work function in a group is perhaps a particular danger of political groupings, whether national or ideological. This may be so because the national or political group's work is less well defined. If scientists in a laboratory, or a group of other workers, were dominated not by the work-function but by psychotic assumptions the actual work could not be performed. This is not so in political groupings, which seem to embody most easily feelings of superiority, messianic mission, convictions of rightness and paranoia about others. This may also be because political groupings have to do with the search for power, which in itself is a primitive aim. It has been said that the tragedy of democracies is that in order to get to the top you must have qualities which make you unfit to be at the top. Of course, this is even more true of dictator ships.

Politics are involved in any sizeable grouping; it is an unrealistic ideal to think that one can have an organisation or society without politics. There will always be different views about policies to be pursued, giving rise to political tensions, and there will also be destructive tensions resulting from personal rivalries and the search for power. But, in an ordinary, well-functioning group those politics will be subordinated to the work-function of the group. One can say 'too much politicking will not be tolerated because it will disrupt the work.' Not so in a political grouping, which has no other task but politics.

A political group may be an organisation, such as a state or political party within a state, but there is a larger, undefined political group which is in fact all of us. Everybody does some political thinking, unavoidably, even those who do not bother with political parties. And our political thinking is largely controlled by the group, for instance the nation-state to which we belong. Unthinkingly we adopt the mental posture of the group we belong to, a posture which may be quite irrational and dangerous for our survival. I think our present nuclear situation produces a constellation in which the deepest psychotic anxieties are aroused and the most primitive psychotic behaviour is used by the group.

Glover wrote in 1946:[40]

The first promise of the atomic age is that it can make some of our nightmares come true. The capacity so painfully acquired by normal man to distinguish between sleep, hallucination, delusion and the objective reality of waking life has for the first time in history been seriously weakened.

A 13 year-old patient of Dr Mack,[64] an American analyst, complained of her difficulty in maintaining the boundary between fantasy and reality in relation to the nuclear threat: 'My imagination scares me. That is one of the things that scares me most. I am still scared of being killed when I am unreasonable but I cannot really categorise nuclear war into what is real death and what could not be.' This followed analysis of her nightmares, her unconscious destructiveness giving rise to nightmare fears (what she called being unreasonable). And she was complaining that she could not differentiate (her word was 'categorise') the nuclear threat from her night-fears.

The existence of the Bomb stirs our destructive megalomania. One of the originators of the atomic weapon, Robert Oppenheimer, described how when watching the first atomic explosion he had an exultant thought: 'I am become death.' None of us is free from the lure of such excitement.

The possibility of implementing our infantile destructive megalomania induces both terror and guilt: guilt, because our own destructive impulses are stirred and we all feel implicated, terror because of the destruction released. Terror is also increased because the most primitive way of dealing with our destructiveness is to project it outside and create monsters.

A clear example of dealing with guilt by projection is the way the Americans and the British, who identify closely with them, deal with the unbearable guilt of having dropped the first atomic bombs. It appears to be the belief of the majority of US and British people that it is all right for us to have atomic weapons since we would never use them unreasonably – not like those 'others' which could be Russians, Arabs or Israelis. This is an amazing claim by the very people who were the first to produce an atomic weapon and the *only* ones to use it: 'Trust me because I'm the only mass murderer in the room'! Yet this is not only the contention of our organised political parties, it also seems to pervade the political thinking of most of our citizens.

The role of projection in political process is well known, but this is not the only dangerous defence mechanism. We can defend ourselves against guilt and terror by actually increasing our megalomania: 'We shall prevail; we do not even need to have a war; we are powerful enough to frighten them.' This is called deterrence. Such megalomanic thinking does not take into account the fact that the frightened enemy may become more, not less, dangerous and bellicose. This is a particular danger today. Suddenly the Soviet Union appears to be weak and frightened; so we can project our own helplessness and fear onto them. We feel great and triumphant: a dangerous political stance, which cuts us off from realities.

Another schizoid defence, which laypeople can easily observe, is depersonalisation. We think in terms of pushing a button to annihilate millions without any sense of those millions being persons, and without any personal responsibility on our part. We rely on computers and then dread that they might start a war, again avoiding any personal involvement. We also have recourse to schizoid withdrawal and apathy. In the political sphere this manifests itself as lack of interest.

Why can't we use our sanity in our political thinking? I think we use group and political processes in a destructive way also by projecting our sanity into the leaders of the group, rather like a child who relies on the parents to keep it safe. We can excuse our own apathy by the thought that we have, particularly in a democracy, elected a government whose task is to look after us. Unfortunately this projection does not work, for the fact is that when a group is dominated by psychotic anxieties and defences it throws up the leaders and governments which best express them! So our governments are no saner than we are. Now we seem to project our sanity into Gorbachev. It does not matter how madly we rearm – he is sane, he will not retaliate, *his* sanity will save us.

All the mechanisms I have described as ruling at the moment our political behaviour and thinking are based on a denial of realities, both external and internal. Our projections, both negative into the enemy and idealising into our own groupings or governments (or even into the enemy in some cases), distort our perception of external reality. The same process of projection keeps us out of touch with our internal realities. It diverts attention from urgent internal problems and conflicts to, instead, an external situation of dealing with enemies. Our projections of hostility keep us unaware of our own aggression, both in fantasy and in reality. This is very important because it is only the awareness of one's own aggression that brings with it the capacity for concern and realistic thinking. The Falklands war, Mrs Thatcher's role in this and what was called the national mood at that time provide many examples of these reality-denying mechanisms.

The dangers that threaten us at the moment are not the forces of nature; they are the dangers we bring on ourselves by our inability to think sanely about political issues. The dangers are of such magnitude now that unless we can apply sanity to political thinking the whole survival of the human race is at risk. That is why I am immensely grateful to the Medical Campaign Against Nuclear Weapons for focussing on this neglected subject.

It is necessary to present people with facts, for instance the fact of what would be the effects of a nuclear conflict – which MCANW and other organisations such as CND are doing admirably. But knowledge of these facts and rational argument, although both essential, are apparently not enough. It is rather like telling a psychotic that he is not in fact Napoleon and trying to prove it to him by facts and rational argument. To help people respond to the facts and the rational arguments we also have to address ourselves to their anxieties and psychological defences, and make insight into those processes more available to peace campaigners and people at large. As psychologists we have only one contribution to make – insight – but this is quite an important one.

Above all we must struggle against the disabling and dangerous effects of group structures, the fetters of group thinking. We must not delegate our feeling and thinking to the dominant group because that makes us thoughtless and truly helpless. We become potential cannon-fodder in a war with no survival.

DISCUSSION

Question: If you get great satisfaction out of working with children, as I do, but are frustrated by the policies imposed on your work, you can only change this by moving away from that work into an administrative or political role. Because women remain more involved with children, whether professionally or domestically, we are more affected by policy-decisions but are less represented amongst decision-makers, who are generally male. How can we deal with this dilemma in the nuclear situation?

Dr Segal: To have influence you must have power. Despite the danger of power corrupting, refusing to take one's power – to take responsibility – is also a terrible mistake. We don't want the situation of Hitler and the holocaust to be repeated, where only a few individuals spoke out against this, and the professional voices that could have warned against what was developing and how it might be averted kept quiet, out of fear of interfering with politics. We should use our professional authority, when we have this. Anyway, the nuclear situation has a great effect on children, so this is rightly a concern of the medical profession.

Air Commodore Mackie: I think the assumption of a centre-periphery split which is behind your question is part of the problem. You are both at the centre and at the cutting edge. Anyone working with children is directly involved in nuclear matters, because the education system introduces them to a bomb culture, a nuclear mentality which is the root of the whole problem. The great controversy a few years ago over peace studies in schools was very significant – this posed a real danger to the system. Without political interference the commonsense and greater humanity of peace studies would have caught on more and more.

Question: How can we bring up children to adopt non-violent values, of compassion and caring, which will help create a conflict-free world for future generations?

Dr Segal: I believe that this is possible, by bringing children up in an atmosphere of tolerance and compassion. But it is not easy, and there are many external influences on them. I don't believe children or anyone can actually be conflict-free; that's a false ideal. We must aim at enabling them to face conflict and deal with it.

Dr Morris Bradley: Perhaps it is not a matter of whether conflict can be eliminated but how we handle conflict. Cooperation is a productive way of handling conflict, of dealing with stress. So we need to place cooperation much more at the centre of education and socialisation. Children will not learn this from lectures and lessons, but by finding through experience that cooperation is a good way to solve many of the difficulties that arise, and by seeing the adults around them doing this routinely and well. Our children will become mediators and peacemakers only if we ourselves do.

Professor Norman Dixon: Hitler's Germany provides a negative example of child-rearing. As Alice Miller describes[70, 71] in Germany before the Second World War a book recommending that children be hurt, humiliated, ridiculed, made to feel guilty and be obedient, went to 40 editions. Its advice to parents produced the Hitler generation and the horrors they were capable of. From this negative example we can gain some idea of what is needed.

*Dr Jim Dyer:** It's been pointed out already that, although peace studies as such have been virtually stopped in schools, there are many other opportunities for teachers to teach and exemplify tolerance, compassion and cooperation, and increase children's self-esteem. Peace studies need not be a separate curricular item, in fact those values should pervade all teaching and all contact with children, whether by teachers or others.

Dr Segal: In terms of positive humanitarian values, Britain seems to be going backwards, not only in how we treat young people but in a harsher adult climate too. At a time when the Soviet Union is moving slowly towards tolerance and freedom, we are moving away from those values.

---

* Dr Jim Dyer chaired one of the discussion sessions at the MCANW Conference.

5

Conflict Dynamics and Conflict Resolution

MORRIS BRADLEY

My assertion is that it is primarily through psychology, in the broadest sense, that we can understand the nuclear confrontation and what needs to be done about it. There is sufficient knowledge to understand why we have created and sustained the nuclear confrontation and – a far more significant claim – to identify precisely the process that has to be applied in order to escape from the present dangers and to reap the immense rewards of peace.

Unfortunately, it is also evident from the research that there are formidable psychological barriers which we have to overcome, both individually and collectively, if this process is to be achieved.

As far back as 1948 a small number of psychologists began to study the nuclear confrontation. Many other psychologists have developed research areas that now can be seen to be directly applicable to the problem. Psychologists such as Frank[35] have shown how deeply our thinking is imprisoned in past experience, leaving us ill-equipped to deal with the rapidity of change and the unprecedented scale of the new realities of the nuclear age. There is now extensive evidence, however, on many aspects of the problem, for example how enmity develops, how our perceptions of other nations are distorted, and how we operate double standards in international affairs.[5,32,75,99]

A major difficulty of my task is that the methods of psychological research are not generally understood, so I must ask the reader to accept that the claims made are based on empirical evidence, typically after decades of research. Here I can only outline one example, chosen because it is quite memorable and can be described briefly; it relates to a very elusive but crucial phenomenon, psychological denial.

The Royal Society of London published the Report of its Study Group on Risk Assessment in 1983.[83] This included research assessing the anxiety of people living at various distances from major hazards such as dams and nuclear power stations. As expected, anxiety increased as the distance from the danger decreased but, contrary to what most people would predict, the amount of anxiety expressed reached a peak at 2 to 4 kilometres and then reduced sharply for those living closest to the danger. From these and many other experiments it seems plausible to conclude not only that humans can be profoundly irrational but also that we have a remarkable capacity for denying realities that are too frightening to admit, suppressing the truth even from ourselves.

Although some people may simply lack the imagination to realise what the nuclear confrontation means, there is evidence that those who do begin to perceive the reality normally develop denial in late childhood in order to cope with everyday life and to avoid the feelings of helplessness and depression that the truth engenders.[2, 16, 78] The strength of this process of denial is not generally recognised, but it is familiar to the medical profession when the question arises of revealing information about incurable illness.

Denial has to be understood in order to realise why so many people behave as if nuclear weapons were not inherently dangerous. Nuclear war is so terrifying a possibility that denial is ubiquitous, even though this terror is partly assuaged by the belief – not necessarily plausible – that nobody could be so insane as to attack if there are sufficiently terrible weapons with which to retaliate. However, when the possibility of nuclear war happening by accident is considered, it must be even more emotionally shocking and subject to denial. The possibility that civilisation could end through blunder is incompatible with the system of beliefs that most people hold about the meaning of life. Our cultural traditions make such a possibility unimaginable for many people. It is easier to deny such an appalling reality than to face the anguish of reconstructing a belief system to accommodate it, and to act upon the implications. The medical profession can try to help to overcome this denial, having more awareness of the fragility of life and, from Darwinian theory, having an understanding of how catastrophic consequences can result entirely from chance processes.

Psychologists developing Festinger's theory argue that those who want to believe that nuclear deterrence keeps them safe (and that is a deep psychological need) must deny that the weapons are inherently dangerous. Yet we know that those who control nuclear weapons believe that they should be used if national interests are threatened, and are trained to launch them on command. In Great Britain, the Prime Minister and other government ministers stated quite explicitly that they would not hesitate to launch a nuclear attack if necessary. These people have full access to information, so we have to ask how they could launch such an arsenal of destruction unless there was psychological denial of responsibility and denial of the magnitude of the consequences.

After more than 40 years' deployment of nuclear weapons, there is evidence from the Canadian Institute for International Peace and Security survey[13] that more than 60 per cent of the public in Canada, Britain and West Germany now say that a nuclear attack is more likely to be launched by accident than by deliberate aggression. This seems to reflect a growing awareness of the risk of accidents, but does not seem to have had a proportionate effect on support for nuclear weapons. Weapons have been so integral a part of our past culture that it is not surprising that deep ambivalence is revealed in opinion polls.[34,80] The public has been told frequently that in order to make deterrence credible, tens of thousands of nuclear weapons are deployed in an immediate state of readiness, capable of being launched with a few minutes' warning. The public has also been given repeated assurances that there is no possibility at all that anything serious could go wrong with any of this destructive capability. That means believing that nuclear weapons are unique, and not subject to accidents, mistakes, wrong decisions, folly, insanity, terrorism, or suicidal revenge. Most people seem to want to believe both of these propositions and typically become emotionally disturbed if the logic is probed. Their ambivalence seems to imply that the need for nuclear weapons to provide a sense of protection is so great that the dangers inherent in the weapons are denied whenever that realisation would force a choice that could include giving up the weapons.

Yet there are people who do grapple with the reality. They realise that it cannot be rational to assert that all of the people who design, build, deploy, test, maintain, control, and make decisions about such weapons are infallible. In fact, many crises, near-accidents and accidents have been documented.[87]

Secrecy is a major problem. For example, the Institute for Policy Studies was only able to discover in 1989 through diligent research and access to records under the United States' Freedom of Information Act that a fire and series of explosions on USS *Belknap* in the Mediterranean in 1975 burned to within 40 feet of the ship's nuclear weapons systems. Since 1945 approximately 1,200 such incidents have been brought to light but the full total, including those attributable to the Soviet Union, must be much greater.

Evidence, summarised by Britten,[10] shows that decisions taken under stress are subject to powerful psychological distortions, so there is a grave danger that those who control nuclear weapons would launch a nuclear war as a result of these and other psychological pressures. This is most likely when decision-time is short and there is a perceived threat. Currently the detection of a nuclear attack leaves only a few minutes for decisions, even if there is no delay in informing the decision-makers. The commander of a submarine or naval task force must face decisions involving nuclear weapons while subject to the additional stresses of implementing complex military commands in a hostile area such as the Persian Gulf, and under pressure from perceived or actual attacks. According to the former spy Oleg Gordievski, a near panic in the Soviet Union on 8–9 November 1983 nearly resulted in an accidental nuclear war. With the leader Chernenko dying and a closed, suspicious atmosphere in the Kremlin, the secret United States military exercise Able Archer seemed to confirm fears that the United States was in the process of launching a pre-emptive nuclear attack.[11]

Research on the nature of risk now emphasises the 'risk equation' in which both the probability of an accident and the severity of its consequences need to be differentiated.[22,33,36] Although an accident with nuclear weapons may appear to be very unlikely, taking the severity of the consequences of such an accident into account means that even a very small probability should be unacceptable. Of course, the risks inherent in the nuclear arsenals vary. There is the risk of releasing clouds of plutonium and other radioactive components without a nuclear detonation; the risk of a single accidental nuclear explosion; the risk of accidentally launching multiple nuclear warheads; and the risk of a full-scale accidental nuclear war.

There is a great deal of psychological evidence showing that anyone will make uncharacteristic, irrational and potentially catastrophic errors in some circumstances. It is precisely because nuclear weapons systems are believed to have been made absolutely safe that the risks of unforeseen human error have become most grave. The ingenuity that is applied to circumventing safety systems in the interests of profit or avoiding work is matched only by the degree of irresponsibility involved. Already accidents at nuclear power plants have shown that assurances by experts in the past that the risks of accidents were so insignificant that they could be ignored were based on flawed assumptions. When human factors are taken into account the probabilities rise alarmingly.

Logic dictates that although improving safety devices and procedures can reduce risks, those associated with a nuclear weapon can only be completely eliminated when that weapon has been dismantled or destroyed. This logic seems to strike great fear in many people, however. For them it seems that even a remote future with significantly fewer nuclear weapons is unimaginable, unattainable or fundamentally undesirable.

The weapons have become such powerful talismans against fear that we cling to them like children in the dark, denying that such a way of seeking protection brings with it unprecedented dangers. For those who can face the reality of the dangers of nuclear weapons, however, only dismantling or destroying a nuclear weapon is an acceptable response to the risks. Their priorities demand that urgent solutions are found for those problems that bar progress in reducing the nuclear arsenals.

Happily, the process by which agreement to dismantle or destroy nuclear weapons can be reached has been thoroughly researched and proved to work in practice in many other contexts. We have the psychologically important precedent of seeing the INF Treaty carried out by both Superpowers. The same process is equally applicable in reducing conventional forces. This process is cooperation, and psychologists and others have convincing evidence about the conditions in which it can be achieved and the ways in which it can be facilitated, including mediation techniques.[4,19,92,95] Since cooperation develops best initially through a series of small increments, the possibility exists that long before the arsenals reach some minimal level of deterrence public attitudes will have changed so profoundly under the influence of the success of cooperation that total elimination of the remaining nuclear and offensive conventional weapons will have become a safe, realistic and attainable goal.

Unhappily, there are major psychological barriers which make people reluctant to attempt cooperation even when the rewards are great and the process is well-understood.[6] The prevailing culture in technologically advanced countries emphasises self-interest and competition. Attitudes that prize most highly the possibility of winning personal gain lead to deep suspicion and are often overtly hostile to the cooperative approach. This is because, for cooperation to be successful, both parties can only gain through the mutual acceptance of equity. The emphasis on winning more than an opponent prevents cooperation and can result in both achieving far less than cooperation offers. Attitudes of rivalry and enmity are counterproductive but they are locked into basic values and beliefs that are primarily acquired through experiences in the formative years of life.[82]

Denial is also a powerful barrier to cooperation, protecting those who fail to cooperate from the painful knowledge of what they have lost through trying to win too much. The psychological way to counteract denial and facilitate cooperation is to make the choices and consequences more explicit, with concrete rather than abstract evidence; to provide a process of mediation and support for the individual's emotional involvement; and to provide a systematic procedure whereby a succession of achievements can be gained, probably in small increments at first, so that realism and success prevail over helplessness and pessimism.

We must also consider the implications of those people who have achieved the most dominant positions in our society, and are likely to be in control of nuclear weapons policy, having typically succeeded through acquiring aggressively competitive values and hostility to cooperation. Such people could not be expected to respond to opportunities to cooperate for mutual advantage nor to be competent in managing the cooperative process. Moreover, by perceiving the world exclusively in terms of confrontation such people are much more likely to make the decision to launch nuclear weapons.

How can we take President Eisenhower's advice and bring the talents of the public to bear upon these crucial decisions? The medical profession, with a value-system so firmly based in care and concern for those in need, clearly has a vital role to play.

From the theory of cooperation, it is clear that nuclear confrontation is a classic case in which cooperation is the optimal, and in the long run, the *only* survival strategy. The inevitable outcome of prolonged confrontation is bleak. The rewards for international cooperation are not restricted to avoiding nuclear catastrophe and saving huge military budgets. Success breeds confidence just as failure breeds helplessness. There is an immense human creative potential waiting to be released once the nuclear threat is eliminated. The profound changes in our attitudes to other nations and the renewed hope for the future will bring about a revival of mutual confidence that will transform human society and bring about nothing less than a new Renaissance.

Science is changing the world so rapidly that it compels a precipitate choice: either to adopt the new mode of international cooperation, or to continue to risk mutual destruction through an inflexible, aggressive stance. Science can provide the means, not only to resolve the nuclear confrontation, but also to deal with the many other urgent problems that cannot be solved without international cooperation.

6

Do the Media Promote a Nuclear Mentality?

JOHN ELDRIDGE

In 1980 UNESCO published the MacBride Report *Many Voices, One World*.[62] This includes discussion of the responsibilities of the media in relation to the goal of peace, with this key paragraph:

> The primary function of the media is always to inform the public of significant facts, however unpleasant or disturbing they may be. At times of tension, the news consists largely of military moves and statements by political leaders which give rise to anxiety. But it should not be impossible to reconcile full and truthful reporting with a presentation that reminds readers of the possibility – indeed the necessity of – peaceful solutions to disputes. We live, alas, in an age stained by cruelty, torture, conflict and violence. These are not the natural human condition; they are scourges to be eradicated. We should never resign ourselves to endure passively what can be cured. Ordinary men and women in every country – and this includes a country depicted as 'the enemy' – share a yearning to live out their lives in peace. That desire, if it is mobilised and expressed, can have an effect on the actions of governments. These statements may appear obvious, but if they appeared more consistently in the media, peace would be safer.

What comes through the MacBride report is a view that stresses the goal of peace as transcending other political and national interests and the need for an active rather than passive acceptance of this goal: 'The spirit of peace and the will to preserve peace must be tirelessly cultivated and consolidated.' The mass media, therefore, are called to a constructive and responsible role in this respect.

How the media in fact live up to these responsibilities is another matter. This was what the UNESCO conference on the media and disarmament met to discuss in Nairobi in 1983. In her background paper 'UNESCO Mass Media Declaration and Disarmament'[77] Dr Breda Pavlic pointed out that military/industrial/political complexes in all parts of the world have a self-preserving and self-reinforcing character:

> They are powerful, resourceful and pervasive coalitions that have developed around the common purpose: the continued expansion of the military sector, irrespective of actual (and not perceived) military needs, and most of all irrespective of their society's real human needs. How much the world's mass media assist them in this either through business links or more-or-less concealed submission to the state-bureaucratic apparatus, remains an open question for the moment.

This reminds us that the mass media are not free-floating institutions independent of the societies in which they are located. They have to survive in an environment that can include a variety of constraints – commercial, political, economic and ideological. In practice news about disarmament may be neglected whilst news which emphasises the need for strong defence may be promoted. For example, the evidence available suggests that both the 1978 and 1983 UN Special Sessions on Disarmament were not well reported in the world's press. On both occasions, however, NATO chose to have its own conference and this was widely reported. If press and broadcasting are tied too closely to a state or party apparatus they may offer plenty of peace talk but their interpretation of events may be narrow, even dogmatic; adversaries within and without that society may be treated as identikit caricatures. In all modern societies the mass media remain a site for cultural struggle.

Those who produce the news output may be constrained by powerful forces but they are not necessarily determined by them. They have the opportunity not only to reflect official definitions of reality but to point to alternative possibilities and proposals. What happens in the space where media messages are articulated matters very much. There can be trivialisation, chauvinism and misinformation. Journalists can be on the receiving end of censorship, disinformation and propaganda campaigns. But if the issue of peace is as significant for the future of the world as the UNESCO position maintains, then all of this is a challenge to media-owners, producers, editors and journalists. In fact this guiding principle enabled the Nairobi conference, consisting of both academics and representatives from the mass media in a large number of countries – East, West, North and South – to reach some general conclusions. The fact that consensus was achieved among such a disparate group of people with differing interests and political perspectives was, in a small way, encouraging.

Because of this recognition of the media's capacity to influence perceptions of threat and conceptions of security, the Nairobi conference argued the need for pluralism in sources of information, including peace and disarmament research institutes, in accordance with the rights of the public in all countries to know and to communicate about the causes and consequences of the arms race and obstacles to disarmament. Journalists everywhere should be enabled to explore disarmament from many approaches, including the links between disarmament and development and emerging new concepts of security. In the exercise of their professional duties they should be enabled to use a variety of relevant sources and apply their critical awareness to them in a constant search for the highest level of accuracy and truth.

The importance of access to diverse sources of information is worth detailing. If restrictions are imposed through press censorship or through journalists relying too extensively on official statements then limits are clearly being placed on the public's right to know. In the Falklands conflict during 1982, for example, foreign correspondents in Britain complained bitterly about their exclusion from press briefings. Many British journalists were deeply unhappy about their treatment by Ministry of Defence officials and the military. More generally the lobby system, which gives special privileges to some correspondents in exchange for non-attributable comments, has been much criticised both for its secrecy, exclusiveness and opportunities for manipulation by government. These and many other aspects of media coverage of the Falklands dispute have been well documented by Richard Harris[49] in his book *Gotcha: The Media, the Government and the Falklands Crisis.*

What this points to is the need for critical journalism – an approach to issues and stories which does not take the official line or the official handout for granted. Alternative sources of information provide some check on the reliability of official information. In defence and disarmament, for example, there are research institutes with specialist academic knowledge, such as the International Institute of Strategic Studies in London, the Stockholm International Peace Research Institute, and the Armament and Disarmament Information Unit of Sussex University in Britain.

The problematic nature of the relationship between journalists and sources is worthy of more attention. Even where attempts are made to manage the relationship for different purposes or interests, the possibility of 'slippage' always exists. A good example occurred in October 1987 when, for the first time, defence correspondents were invited by the Ministry of Defence to visit the Royal Navy nuclear depot at Coulport (on Loch Long, Scotland). This is where Polaris missiles are serviced, fitted and loaded, and where facilities for the Trident missile intended to replace Polaris are being developed. Although the Ministry of Defence no doubt had their own public relations purposes for the visit, questions were raised which proved embarrassing to the government. The main point to emerge was that, unlike the present arrangements for Polaris, Coulport will be no more than a storage facility for Trident; the servicing and maintenance will be done at the US Navy base in Kings Bay, Georgia. This led David Fairhall[31] the *Guardian* defence correspondent to write:

> The Ministry of Defence objects, quite understandably, to this being described as 'rent-a-missile', or more provocatively, 'rent-a-deterrent'. But the impression it made on the naval officials concerned can be judged from the picture of a Trident missile that was posted up with the Hertz logo pasted on it.

He went on to describe it as 'a Black and Decker deterrent' – you hand your old tool in to the shop and get a reconditioned one in exchange. All this raised for Fairhall much larger questions about the real status of Britain's independent nuclear deterrent: 'Here is yet another example, in other words, of the extent to which the United Kingdom has become the military dependent of its big ally across the water.' This had parliamentary repercussions with the Foreign Secretary trying to defuse the row and Ministry of Defence officials in London disowning the official briefing which the defence correspondents had received in Scotland. This illustrates the problem of slippage and the inherent difficulties of managing news entirely to one's intentions not least because, while there may be disparities in power relations between government and press, those who publish still have the power to unsettle if they choose to use it.

It was argued in conclusion at the UNESCO conference that the media have the capacity to influence perceptions of threat and contribute to the formation of attitudes concerning security. For example, there is a strong contrast between the doctrines of deterrence espoused by the great powers and the views expressed in the UN Special Session on Disarmament in 1978. This stated that the accumulation of nuclear arms leads to greater insecurity and that a programme of disarmament is needed to promote lasting international security. If the deterrence view becomes part of the taken-for-granted reality which the media portray then perceptions of threat will be shaped by that assumption. Similarly the conference drew attention to the Palme Commission's report *Common Security*[76] since it challenges received notions of deterrence, mutual assured destruction and first-strike capacity. Palme was quite specific about this, arguing that international security must rest on a commitment to joint survival rather than on a threat of mutual destruction. The Commission programme contained well developed proposals for reducing the arms race and establishing new collective security procedures. Unless proposals of this type are seriously covered in the media we may lose sight of what Gwyn Prins[79] has called the paradox of security:

The paradox of security is not only that in the nuclear world those habits of mind and expressions of power to which we are accustomed are no longer consistent with security, even in its restricted form of defence. Were it merely so the situation would only be unfortunate rather than grave, and it would be stable. The paradox is bitter because the relationship between nuclear weapons and security is volatile and corrosive. It is an inverse relationship: the more that people and states seek to increase their security by the old methods, but with the new atomic power, the less security they have; and the more that heightened insecurity is sensed the faster the arms race becomes, the heavier the burden, and the more hateful, aggressive, expansionist and devious the enemy appears. In this way the spiralling accelerates viciously and the hope of escape recedes as the nuclear presence spreads over the whole political landscape.

In a curious twist of events, however, the American military applied some of the British experience of the Falklands and the media when they invaded the British Commonwealth island of Grenada in 1983. A total news black-out operated – no members of the press went in with the first or second wave of troops and in fact four members of the press (including one from the *Washington Post*) were taken off the island by the military and were kept incommunicado for 18 hours; even after that they were not able to get their stories back. So what the US public (and the world) received from Grenada was only official military film. This has served to underline the conflicts of interest that, whether real or perceived, are judged by the military to exist between them and the media. Television in particular is seen as a suspect medium. Although the correctness of the view may be challenged, there is a widely held opinion that the Vietnam war was much affected by the presence of television. If the television news which brought the horrors of war into the homes of millions of Americans night after night was held responsible for undermining belief in the war effort and shifting public opinion against the war, then television could be seen as a hostile witness by the military.

What about the overarching question of the nuclear arms race and the problems of disarmament? There is an argument that suggests that with a plurality of media outlets all sides of the question can and do get represented. This may be formally true yet over the years television programmes that have been the subject of bans and postponements have usually been from the standpoint of the peace movement. There was the long-running saga of 'The War Game' which was made for the BBC by Peter Watkins some 25 years ago and only recently shown. (It was shown privately, as a film, in many places in Britain during that time.) An invitation to Professor E.P. Thompson to give the Dimbleby lecture was withdrawn as a result of a veto by Ian Trethowan, BBC's then Director General. John Pilger's documentary on the arms race 'The Truth Game' was delayed in its screening until his 'personal view' could be 'balanced' against Max Hastings' 'personal view' in 'The War About Peace'. If Hastings' documentary had been made first would there have been a mirror-image controversy about the need for balance? It is the views which challenge the conventional wisdom that have to be balanced, rather than views which underline and justify it. Or, if such views do get through, there may be other consequences. In 1982 the psychologist Nicholas Humphrey delivered the Bronowski lectures in which he argued the case for nuclear disarmament. The Bronowski lectures were discontinued. Mrs Bronowski commented: 'I could have told you five minutes after the lecture that there'd never be another one. I think basically it's a political thing.'

Nevertheless, during the 1980s there have been many programmes in Britain – current affairs, documentaries, debates – that have given serious attention to the nuclear arms race. In the period leading up to the deployment of Cruise and Pershing missiles, for example, there were significant contributions from TV programmes in Britain such as *Panorama, World in Action, Weekend*

World, QED and *Everyman*. The *Everyman* programme produced a film report by Peter France on the World Council of Churches' session on nuclear weapons and Christian conscience held in Amsterdam in November 1981. Again, as public discussion moved away from Cruise and Pershing and on to the Strategic Defence Initiative, *Panorama* produced a forceful documentary by Tom Mangold entitled 'Beyond Deterrence'. In it, and an article in the *Listener*, the rationality of the arms race and the direction it was taking were severely questioned.

So there is some diversity and some pluralism in the kinds of subjects covered and perspectives from which they are covered. But difficulties do arise. Censorship and blocking of programmes does occur, albeit in somewhat erratic and arbitrary ways, telling us something about the limits of dissent and of the political pressures that can be exerted. It is salutary to recall, for instance, that while Duncan Campbell's programme on the Zircon satellite (in the *Secret Society* series) has now been shown on BBC television the other programme 'Cabinet' has not. This included an account of the way in which a disinformation campaign was coordinated within Whitehall against the peace movement leading up to the 1983 British General Election. These are serious matters in a society which is formally committed to democratic values.[25]

Within our society, the mass media operate in the context of a deterrence culture. Security against attack, the need for nuclear deterrence, the enemy threat and the danger of 'one-sided disarmament' all coalesce. Hence peace studies are routinely described as unilateralist indoctrination by those on the political right. Yet the inbuilt instabilities of deterrence are passed over by such people and the real status of Britain's 'independent' deterrent left unexamined. For example, wherein lies the British deterrent's independence and under what possible circumstances could the weapons be used to defend us? These are not questions which are regularly addressed in the British media. Yet as the World Council of Churches' statement[39] from Vancouver in 1983 noted:

Nuclear deterrence can never provide the foundation for genuine peace. It is the antithesis of an ultimate faith in that love which casts out fear. It escalates the arms race in a vain pursuit of stability. It ignores the economic, social and psychological dimensions of security and frustrates justice by maintaining the status quo in world politics ...

In the wake of the INF Treaty and the actual dismantling of nuclear weapons in East and West, the mass media have a crucial role to play in keeping us informed about the progress, problems and negotiations on nuclear weapons. If, for example, the British government wants to promote weapons' modernisation programmes which would or might have the effect of circumventing the INF agreement, then we should be told. Arms control and questions of nuclear disarmament can be complicated at the level of detail and it is all too easy for us to be fobbed off with public relations packages designed to massage public opinion – to manipulate rather than to inform. We do know that the Soviet Union is no longer regarded as a military threat by the majority of British people and this might make it harder for the government to sustain the deterrence culture to which it still seems wedded. In all of this the media, not least public service broadcasting (whose own future is now more problematical), have a heavy responsibility laid upon them. They have to operate on the basis that the government interest is not always identical with the public interest. We must judge their performance by the way they respond to this considerable challenge.

If we are to go beyond rhetoric and speak with any confidence about a free press in a free society, then we must take it as axiomatic that such a press will not merely reproduce the thoughts, opinions and assumptions of the powerful but also analyse and, where necessary, question them, and present alternatives fairly. On matters concerning war and peace this responsibility and duty could not be more clear.

DISCUSSION

Question: I have been studying how the award of the Nobel Peace Prize to IPPNW (International Physicians for the Prevention of Nuclear War) was reported. I found a distinct difference between the reports of named correspondents and those from press agencies. The named press reports were either reasonably neutral or their unfavourable bias was fairly apparent. But the press agency reports were uniformly hostile, and in a pervasive, subtle way which was harder to detect and discount. Why would this be?

Professor Eldridge: When the Glasgow Media Group first started monitoring TV news programmes we were surprised how similar the news was on the different channels. When for example we examined media reporting of the UN Special Session on Disarmament in 1982 we found the same phrases were being used, even the same sentences, on different channels. The same news agencies were providing the same selections from the same speeches which were then broadcast on a multiplicity of programmes, with minor differences of final editing; this is not a true diversity of information – it only gives that surface impression. Much of the reporting was also curiously uninformative. A tremendous filtering went on: no speeches from non-governmental organisations and none from Third World countries. Even reports of President Reagan's speech were slanted so as to tell us little or nothing about his position on arms control. Instead they concentrated on the enemy image of the Soviet Union he was building up at the time. At the very least journalists should make clear that they are being selective, and from what point of view.

Question: Why is it that the great range of views concerning nuclear weapons is reflected so poorly in the media? And what can we do about it?

Professor Eldridge: Particularly on TV the range of opinions on any particular issue is usually defined in party-political terms. Of course, this narrows the area of debate and excludes many other opinions; it also tends to reinforce the roles of existing political parties and prevent change. But you can see why – the views of political parties are usually fairly well defined and set out. This makes them an easier framework for the media to operate within. How do we change this? Well, a great deal of tenacity is called for. One method is to use the orthodoxy's arguments in such a way as to open up the debate. For example SDI, Reagan's Star-Wars: in explaining the attractions and need for SDI the media made clear the insecurity of relying on the nuclear deterrent to keep peace forever. After all, if deterrence is as stable and certain as has been claimed for so long, why do we need SDI? Those sort of contradictions allow us to take the initiative, and to work from within the consensus to change it. Similarly with changes in the USSR and Gorbachev's popularity in Western Europe, the media can be challenged much more effectively when their uncritical treatment of nuclear orthodoxy results in reinforcing old Cold War attitudes. The issues of defence, security and international relations are in the process of being redefined, they're beyond the limits of party-political debate now, so there is much more chance of getting new and challenging ideas expressed, although it still takes persistence and good preparation.

Helena Kennedy:* As a barrister I have often worked with the media, and I've come to realise that programmers are in fact responsive in some ways to the public. But we often don't make enough use of this, by phoning and writing in. Certainly we don't make known our views and our dissatisfaction with much reporting as well as right-wing, pro-nuclear groups do. Complaints really are registered by BBC and ITV and they do have a cumulative effect. Where a substantial body of opinion persistently makes itself known to the programme-makers, they do eventually take notice.

Question: Mrs Thatcher often says 'we need the nuclear – nuclear deters, conventional doesn't.' No interviewer ever follows the logic of this and says to her 'if that applies to us why not to every other country. Do you think the world would be safer if every country followed your reasoning?' Why do they miss these obvious follow-up questions?

Professor Eldridge: Very occasionally someone does follow up replies like that. I remember an Australian interviewer who took Mrs Thatcher on simply by being persistent, insisting on a straight answer and exploring the consequences of what she'd said; the uncertainty and hesitation she revealed were very illuminating. This shows how timid most of our media are, and how it is in contrast to this that politicians appear decisive, certain, etc. Many of these interviews are set-piece affairs, with carefully pre-selected interviewers, the favourite ones. The major failure to follow up an important issue that amazes me is Britain's so-called independent deterrent. There is so much to explore here – our dependence on the USA for targeting information, for maintenance and repairs, the constraints of our NATO commitments. But when did you last hear an incisive analysis of this fundamental issue? Meanwhile news broadcasts continue to refer uncritically to 'the independent deterrent' as if it were an unquestionable fact which, of course, they are gradually making it.

It's worth taking note of the type of question asked in in.erviews. Questioning can be of the open 'tell me your views' variety, which at least is clearly uncritical, or of the more subtle 'prompt' variety where the interviewer asks about the next topic he or she knows the interviewee wants to make a point about. Or it may be 'devil's advocate' questioning. This is almost always directed towards people whose views seem to challenge the status quo; their credentials and sincerity are almost always questioned, while interviewees trotting out the received wisdom tend to get uncritical, collusive questioning from the media.

Dr Frank Barnaby: One of the problems is that we often don't see clearly what exactly is the salient point to question. For example, the peace movement has focussed very much on the INF Treaty, and now on START. But these measures won't stop the new nuclear arms race! In fact you can see these protracted talks as distractions which keep our attention from the greatest danger – the current escalation of the arms race. Those treaties will not stop this, and anyway they will take years to implement. What we should be drawing public attention to is the so-called modernisation of nuclear weapons and the new technologies which are both creating a nuclear war-fighting, first-strike capability, with strategies being developed to fit those weapons. Yet too often we continue to argue about policies which have already been superseded, like deterrence based on Mutual Assured Destruction.

A paradox is that new military technologies which are so destabilising when applied to nuclear weapons could enable conventional weapons to become much more effective in defence. So defence could become more cost-effective than offence. This removes the last excuse for having any offensive conventional capability. We could be restructuring our forces to give both greater defence-efficiency and less risk simply by adopting these new technologies in a different way.

* Helena Kennedy chaired the session of the MCANW Conference in which this discussion took place.

7

The Assumptions of Nuclear Weapons Decision-makers

SCILLA ELWORTHY, JOHN HAMWEE and HUGH MIALL

Decisions affecting the future of the world are made by a comparatively small number of people – probably not more than 700 East and West.[12, 67, 69] For six years now the Oxford Research Group has been interested in this human side of the arms race – how the decisions on nuclear weapons are made and by whom they are made, and has published four books on the subject.[26,27,67,69]

This paper describes the assumptions made by a small group of influential British nuclear weapons decision-makers, as revealed in a research project undertaken recently by the Oxford Research Group.

These assumptions are rarely revealed in official publications that explain or support those decisions. But without knowing what the assumptions are it is impossible to test the validity of the decision-makers' arguments, nor to know what kind of debate with them is likely to be fruitful.

We wanted to know if those who make nuclear weapons decisions share a distinctive approach to, and form of reasoning about, nuclear weapons issues, and if so, how that approach could be characterised. A good deal can be gleaned from published documents but it is hard to infer from them the beliefs, values and assumptions which form such a crucial framework for the reasoning. This research set out to uncover the framework.

We interviewed 13 people, nine of whom have played important roles in decisions resulting in nuclear weapons now deployed or soon to be deployed in the UK. We will refer to these nine as 'the decision-makers'. Two obvious points arise. The first is that they are not named here. One interview was granted on a strictly non-attributable basis while others gave us various degrees of freedom to quote and attribute. It seems simplest not to name any of them, and we don't believe this affects our conclusions. The second point concerns the size of the sample. It is impossible to estimate exactly how many people could be called decision-makers by our criteria, but we accept that the sample is small. However, policy-making in government and large organisations operates by consensus around the prevailing orthodoxy. One decision-maker said of this process in the Ministry of Defence:

> I think it's an extremely rational process in so far as you could design a system for optimising the view of a huge organisation, but one which is precisely designed not to challenge the underlying assumptions, to take them as your starting point, the water in which you swim.

In addition, nuclear defence policy in the UK has been bipartisan for virtually the past 40 years, so anyone who is now in a senior position has been deeply influenced by continual contact with that orthodoxy. The questions we asked were not about the details of policy, on which there might be disagreement, but on basic issues such as the purpose of defence policy, the nature of the threat it guards against, the meaning of stable deterrence, and so on. We interviewed at least one person in each of the following categories: the military, scientists, defence contractors, civil servants, and politicians. For all these reasons we conclude that although the sample is small it is broadly representative.

The Decision-makers

Before turning to an analysis of the findings, we think it is worth trying to give some impression of the decision-makers. Having met them, it seems to us a distortion of what we learnt to present their views in an entirely abstract and bloodless way. What follows is a brief portrait of a politician, a civil servant and a scientist.

We waited for the politician in a formal meeting room, luxuriously and elegantly furnished. He sat not in but across a chair, and shifted his position throughout the discussion. It seemed as if he would rather have paced up and down but felt obliged to be confined to a chair. He was very confident, quite clear that he'd thought it all out, he saw no reason to doubt or reconsider, and indeed what he said was always coherent, forceful and frank. He was impatient with generalised academic questions, for example about the nature of decision-making, and preferred to speak very personally, telling stories and anecdotes about his own experience. As the interview ended he pointed to each of us and said, 'Now you're a unilateralist and you're a multi-lateralist.' We replied, truthfully, 'Wrong way round.' He minded that he'd got it wrong.

The civil servant met us in his office at the top of a large government building. He sat full square in his chair, occasionally putting the fingertips of his hands together, but otherwise not moving throughout the interview. You wouldn't take him, on casual acquaintance, to be a powerful man, but in a meeting he would stand out quickly as determined, persistent and clever. He is an intellectual, enjoying and responding to discussion or difficult points. He spoke precisely and without hesitation, colouring his replies with the occasional vivid image and flippant remark. Although you felt he would be unfailingly kind and courteous to anybody, you also felt that he would only be at ease in very restricted circles of the Establishment.

The scientist had huge charm, a good deal of which came from a cheerful and scathing iconoclasm. You felt he'd enjoyed, in equal measure, blowing up fallacious scientific theories and stuffy committee meetings. He'd breezed through work others had found difficult, and done it by retaining a kind of innocent enjoyment in the hunt for what made sense, what worked. His office was messy, piles of paper interspersed with models of inventions, and it was dominated by a huge whiteboard fully filled with formulae and diagrams. It was a place where a lot of work had been done, a lot of problems had been thrashed out, and out of which not a few employees had reeled feeling pretty foolish. He spoke his mind; to one question his reply was 'How am I supposed to answer that question? What an odd question to ask me.' He always spoke colloquially – 'I dunno' was his answer to another. Above all he gave the impression that anything could be done, anything. Not because he is a crusader, determined to achieve a goal, but as an inventor, determined to make it work.

Two general remarks about the group as a whole: the decision-makers, with one notable exception, were well informed and produced coherent and well-argued cases for their views, showing a willingness to consider and reflect on new points. Secondly, when talking about nuclear war many of the decision-makers, in strong contrast to the clear language they normally used, slipped into a kind of childish banter. One referred to radioactive fallout as a 'cloud of gubbins'. Another said '... what you actually do if there is a hostile Russian military move and you don't want to destroy the world, or you don't want to destroy the world before next Thursday ... ' Another referred to the possibility of using British tactical nuclear weapons in the course of battle in Germany and then added 'one might decide on the day that "not tonight Josephine" was the right answer'- a curiously flippant phrase with a rather peculiar conjunction of sex and nuclear war, which has been noted elsewhere.[15]

Their Assumptions

The interviews contain a wealth of statements of fact, beliefs, values, conjecture, perceptions, attitudes, guesses, prejudice, hypothesis and some nonsense. We have concentrated on the assumptions made by these decision-makers. We use the term 'assumption' to mean 'the taking of anything for granted as the basis of argument or action' (*Shorter Oxford English Dictionary*, 1973), and this definition covers what are often called beliefs as well as assumptions. For example, the fact that there has been no war between the nuclear powers in the last 40 years is often used as part of any argument to support the possession of nuclear weapons. Implicit in that argument is the view that nuclear weapons have been responsible for preventing war: such a view could be called either an assumption or belief. Here we use the term 'assumption' to cover both.

A good deal of the argument about nuclear weapons ignores the assumptions made by both proponents and opponents. This is because assumptions are, to a greater or lesser extent, hidden from view. They may be starting points in a chain of reasoning, not elaborated because they seem obvious or uncontentious, or they may never have been fully articulated by the decision-maker. An example is the assumption that different ideologies are the source of conflict and threat between nations. Assumptions may also be unstated links in a chain of reasoning. For example, between the premise that our enemies have nuclear weapons and the conclusion that therefore we must have nuclear weapons lie a host of assumptions, one of which is that nuclear weapons are the best form of defence against nations possessing nuclear weapons.

Assumptions may also be hidden in the use of images, analogies and metaphors: for example, a number of the decision-makers justify the possession of nuclear weapons as an 'insurance policy'. The analogy assumes that the possession of nuclear weapons creates no risk for the possessor, just as the payment of an insurance premium creates no risk for the policy holder. Simple omission of potentially relevant ideas may also be evidence of an assumption. In the course of long and wide-ranging discussion of the issues surrounding nuclear weapons only one of the decision-makers mentioned the public or public opinion at all. This suggests that most of them assume public support for, or indifference to, what they do. Most hidden of all are assumptions arising from the very structure of the decision-makers' arguments and beliefs: the relations they conceive between threat and deterrence, between defence and international relations, and between the existence of conflicts and ways of resolving them.

All these are good reasons why we chose to focus on assumptions. But the best reason is to try and understand, in Philip Larkin's words, 'how we got it':[57]

> ... Where do these
> Innate assumptions come from? Not from what
> We think truest, or most want to do:
> Those warp tight shut, like doors. They're more a style
> Our lives bring with them: habit for a while,
> Suddenly they harden into all we've got
> And how we got it ...

The next sections contain a search for the most important assumptions made by the decision-makers, those which underlie how they think about nuclear weapons and hence, in some degree, how we've got them.

Express Assumptions

These are the common assumptions which the decision-makers are perfectly aware they are making. We call them 'common' both because we encountered them often and because most decision-makers agreed with each other on them. By far the most specific assumption is that

> ... the idea of us ceasing to be a nuclear power and having our next door neighbour, 22 miles across the Channel, in possession of these weapons is unthinkable. You couldn't have a situation where we willingly and freely abandoned Europe to our friendly neighbours, the French. That's prejudice. I certainly believe it.

This is unusual in its open and robust language and in its admission of prejudice, but the point was clearly present in the minds of most decision-makers. At its most sophisticated, this assumption forms part of a complex argument. It is that Europe may not be able to rely on the United States to defend it against a Soviet attack, because that might risk a nuclear attack on the United States itself; therefore Europe must have its own nuclear weapons. Why these must be held by the UK, and not by France alone, entails another assumption:

> ... given history, the fact that we are a nuclear power, the part that we currently play in the world ... quite a significant political power, it is right that we should continue to play the main part in the deterrence of war in Europe through the possession of nuclear weapons.

In summary, these assumptions are modern versions of the following famous comment of the British Foreign Secretary in 1946. When arguing for a British-designed and -built nuclear weapon he said 'We've got to have a bloody Union Jack flying on top of it.'

The next set of assumptions concerns the threat to the UK: that is, the threat against which we need military defences. All agree that there is no immediate threat from the Soviet Union: 'I'm quite clear that my answer, even pre-Gorbachev, to "are the Russians likely to want to attack the West in your lifetime?" is "No".'

However all the decision-makers agree that the Soviet Union remains a threat:

> The threat, I think, is simply that there are people whose views differ widely enough from ours for there to be a risk over time, and I'm talking about a long time ... that if bashing us over the head became an easily available option for dealing with the things they disagree with us about we couldn't be sure they wouldn't.

These decision-makers see the Soviet Union as a threat essentially because of its ideology, by which most decision-makers mean a general belief in a collectivist organisation of society. For a few it means the official, if rather outdated, mission to spread communism throughout the world. One decision-maker saw the Soviet Union as a long-term threat for a rather different reason: 'I see the danger coming about as a result of internal problems in the Soviet Union ... Eventually the Soviet Empire will collapse, as all empires do, and that is the moment of peril ...'

Given that the Soviet Union presents a threat, but not an immediate threat, it is striking that the decision-makers still draw the conclusion that the UK's nuclear weapons must be maintained and modernised now. Some of them say they see the prospect of a general reduction in the numbers of nuclear weapons in the world, but none of them drew the conclusion that this absence of an immediate threat might provide an opportunity to bring about change in the security situation in Europe, and hence in British defence policy.

This point leads to the next group of explicit assumptions. It is that between nuclear weapons states or alliances 'war is unthinkable' or 'war simply isn't on.' This assumption is buttressed in a number of different ways by different decision-makers. The most often mentioned is the assumption that nuclear weapons have kept the peace in Europe:

> ...they know that we know exactly where the Kremlin would go in the event of a crisis ... and they know we can destroy it. That's why we have peace. I actually do believe that's why we have peace, because they know that we can destroy the command and control structure of the Soviet Union in the event of war.

In addition, for war to be 'unthinkable' it is also necessary to be sure that a minor conflict or border skirmish doesn't escalate into war, and that the use of battlefield nuclear weapons doesn't lead to a full-scale exchange of nuclear weapons. Most are confident: 'I don't see escalation as being inevitable, I think it's inconceivable to me.'

A number of others expressed some unease about this and one disagreed: 'I think if the crunch comes it'll go all the way. I'm afraid I do think that.' At this point there is no clear dividing line between escalation and accidental nuclear war. No specific questions were asked about escalation, but no decision-maker mentioned it as a danger. Behind the assumption that neither escalation nor accidental war can happen lies a deeper assumption that, in times of crisis, decision-makers will be in control of what happens on the putative battlefield:

> ... the leaders on both sides would be sufficiently aware of the consequences that they would maintain closer touch with each other than they were able to then [during the Cuban crisis] and I think they would keep the situation under control.

Finally, we come to the assumption that nuclear deterrence is stable. This was explicitly referred to by all decision-makers. 'I believe we are in a very stable condition now; we can probably make it marginally more stable, 99.95 [per cent] can become 99.97 [per cent].'

Stable deterrence needs, in the view of the decision-makers, two things. First it needs stable borders: all the decision-makers agreed that 'Good fences make good neighbours':

> ... the Helsinki agreement on the inviolability of frontiers which I think is extremely important ... plus the existence of a very clear demarcation line between the two [blocs] so that each knows what he must not transgress if he is not to enter into an area of high danger.

Stable deterrence also needs an approximate balance of nuclear weapons held by potential adversaries: a balance which it is the business of decision-makers the world over to preserve. Nearly all the decision-makers accept that such a balance could be found with lower levels of weapons, but they are also clear that it requires the continual modernisation of nuclear weapons:

> Once I'd made up my mind that the thing made sense [a nuclear defence policy] and that we have to carry on, we have to modernise; because without modernisation we weren't credible ... a credible response means that it's got to be the most modern, the most up-to-date ...

On this last point the decision-makers' assumption presents a difficulty: how do you preserve stability by producing weapons of ever greater accuracy, penetration and destructive power? Indeed those decision-makers who believe in both the stability of deterrence and the need to modernise nuclear weapons find a similar difficulty in discussing the rationality of decision-making. One decision-maker said: 'My perception of it [defence decision-making] is that it's fairly rational ... by comparison with most human activities that I'm aware of, it's got its full due of rationality.'

While also accepting that 'The numbers [of nuclear weapons] have become ridiculous haven't they?', another echoed these views: 'It's about as highly rational as one could possibly devise', but then went on to say of the numbers of weapons: ... 'then we're collectively in the mad-house, which in one sense of course we are: we all know that. It's scarcely credible to your Martian that we've piled up nuclear weapons over the last 40 years, for example.'

This assumption of rationality is crucial to stable deterrence.

Only if your enemy is rational in the way that you are rational will he refuse to risk any attack or incursion in the face of your nuclear weapons; only if he is rational will he be deterred. Yet somehow, at the same time, this rationality seems to have put us collectively in the mad-house.

Implicit Assumptions

First, we need to explain how we can assert the existence of implicit assumptions: after all, we cannot use quotations as direct evidence. We used a technique called cognitive mapping[3,24] which provides a graphic representation of the structure of a decision-maker's views.

Each map representing the views of each decision-maker is different. Some of these differences are due, no doubt, to the fact that no two interviews can be the same, and still more to the different weight each individual places on certain aspects of the nuclear issue. Nevertheless there seemed to us to be sufficient common ground to produce one map, which contains a common core of statements and relationships which are present in all the separate maps. This is Figure 7.1.

In Figure 7.1 the arrows represent links between statements. The link may be causal, for example 'a commitment to first use' causes 'an adversary to believe we would use nuclear weapons'; or the link may be logical, for example 'decision-makers are in control' therefore 'the likelihood of unintentional war is small'. The plus and minus signs by the arrows express the nature of the link between two statements: the plus sign signifies that any change in one statement will lead to a similar change in the other. So the greater the commitment to first use, the more an adversary will believe we would use nuclear weapons; conversely, the less the commitment, the less the adversary's belief. The minus sign signifies the opposite. That is, the more decision-makers are in control the less the likelihood of unintentional nuclear war or, conversely, the greater the likelihood of such war.

Figure 7.1 represents the system of thought within which information is interpreted and particular decisions made. It certainly leaves out a lot but we doubt whether it includes anything to which any of them would take exception. As you would expect, it confirms a number of the statements made earlier: stable deterrence is the focal point, and the Soviet threat is prominent. The importance of the rationality of decision-makers is displayed, too, in its links with stable deterrence, and the prevention of unintentional war and escalation.

Figure 7.1 A Cognitive Map of the Assumptions of British Nuclear Weapons Decision-makers

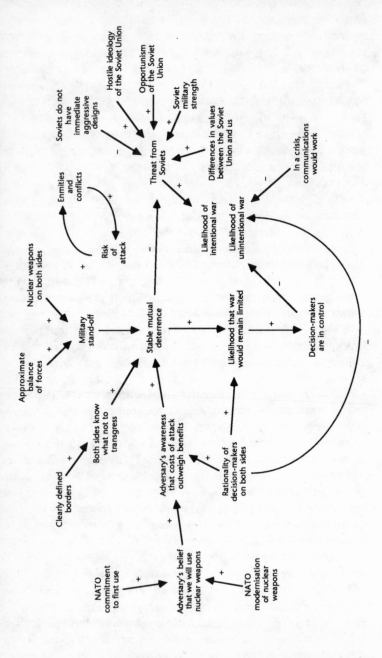

More interesting are the conclusions that can be drawn about implicit assumptions. At its most obvious level, the decision-makers omit to mention two aspects of nuclear weapons which are uppermost in the minds of their critics. The first is the moral or ethical issue, which was only expressly referred to by two decision-makers. One said 'I don't think I ever saw the moral argument.' The other took a rather different line:

> If you were to say to me 'which of the arguments or the sets of arguments used by opponents of nuclear weapons appeals to me most?' I would say 'the moral argument against them' which I'd hope that I do take seriously, which I believe that I've wrestled with a good deal, even though at the end of the day I've come out the other way.

The second omission is the public and the role of public opinion. It was mentioned by only one decision-maker:

> ... the value to my mind of the adoption of flexible response is that it makes the mobilisation of public support for a nuclear defence policy easier ... you have to have a degree of public support for the policy and the mobilisation of that support is, I believe, easier because of the doctrine of flexible response.

Although the thrust of this comment is towards influencing public opinion, the speaker clearly recognises that the whole set of beliefs and assumptions depends on a degree of public support. As for the others, they assume either that the public supports the overall picture set out in Figure 7.1, or that public opinion does not impinge on nuclear weapons policies. Turning from these omissions of statements which one might have expected to see, there are also omissions of links one might have expected to see. There is no link drawn, for example, from Soviet military strength to NATO modernisation of nuclear weapons. It is likely that, if asked specifically, the decision-makers would all draw such a link. Some might see it as a one-way link: Soviet military strength causes NATO to modernise; and some might have seen a two-way link: NATO modernisation also causes an increase in Soviet military strength. That second link does have rather awkward implications – that NATO modernisation increases the threat from the Soviets. This is speculation; but in the course of talking separately about the threat on the one hand and about the Soviet belief that we would use nuclear weapons on the other, the connection was not explicitly made by any decision-maker. Can inferences be drawn from this? One possible inference is that the decision-makers do not see NATO as a threat to the Soviet Union: hence they do not see that the Soviet actions may be taken not in furtherance of their 'hostile ideology' or 'opportunism' but in response to the actions of NATO. It is not possible to be certain if this particular inference is fair, but there is evidence to support a more general inference.

This more general inference is that those who take decisions about vastly complex issues find that complexity daunting, and they seek to simplify. There is a large literature about decision-making where the subject-matter of decisions is both complex and uncertain; criteria which apply to this area.[86] One very common finding is that decision-makers, in order to make decisions at all, have to reduce that complexity.[91] Typically the way they do this is to omit feedback effects, those mutually interacting chains of cause and effect which cause the complexity.[3] It is hard enough for the human brain to grasp a long straight chain of logic or causation, but impossible if there are many feedback effects.

Another missing link is rather more difficult to see in Figure 7.1. It is that the link from stable deterrence to Soviet threat is one-way only. That captures the decision-makers' view that the more stable is deterrence the less strong is the Soviet threat. On the other hand deterrence appears to be unaffected by any change in the level of Soviet threat; this is the missing link. Does it matter that this link is missing?

At first sight it is at least surprising. A lay view would probably be that deterrence is more stable if the threat is reduced. Deterrence may well work at times of great crisis but it is tempting to say that it is more likely to work, or works better, when there is little threat of conflict. But the decision-makers do not appear to make this link. In fact, if you look closely at the map, it becomes clear why they don't. Stable deterrence is maintained by nuclear weapons on both sides, approximate balance of forces, clearly defined borders, NATO commitment to first use, NATO modernisation and the rationality of decision-makers. Of these only 'approximate balance of forces' could be directly affected by a reduction in the threat, specifically the reduction of Soviet military strength. It is quite clear that such a reduction would not have any real effect on stable deterrence – there are so many other factors maintaining it. In short, it is reasonable to infer that the decision-makers assume that stable deterrence must be maintained whatever the level of threat.

This inference is supported by the explicit statement of one of them: 'I'm arguing that we've got to try and make this work [stable deterrence] for the rest of human history.' This might be an uncontentious view if stable deterrence did not involve nuclear weapons on both sides, modernisation and a NATO commitment to first use. It may also be disputed by those who assume that measures of cooperation and trust-building with the Soviet Union over a period of time offer the best route to measures of nuclear disarmament.

One final point about Figure 7.1: underlying all of it is a conception of nation-states acting as if they were rational individuals – pursuing their own goals, recognising borders, being aware that costs outweigh benefits, and so on. This in itself is an assumption about how nation-states decide and act; there are other views.[1] One in particular sees the actions of a nation as a result of a whole tumult of domestic and international pressures, factions, compromises and power struggles.[47] The outcome of this mixture is not necessarily rational, nor what anyone expected or wanted. As one decision-maker said:

> ... nuclear weapons no longer become as expensive or difficult or rare as one had thought as late as 1952/3. And before you know where you were, you looked round and suddenly we have 2,000 tactical nuclear weapons in Europe that the generals had never asked for, the scientists didn't know what they did, and the politicians didn't know what the hell they were for ...

If there is any truth in that view, it challenges the assumption underlying the whole of Figure 7.1 that any nation involved in this process will see the issues in the same rational way and be able to act according to that logic.[81] This time at the national rather than the international level, we come face to face with the uncomfortable observation that we may be 'collectively in the mad-house'.

Controversy

We thought it would be useful to test our view of the importance of these explicit and implicit assumptions. We interviewed two people with considerable knowledge of these issues who have concluded that they cannot support a nuclear defence policy. We asked similar questions of them; if they agreed with the decision-makers then clearly we couldn't maintain that the decision-makers think about these issues in a distinctive way or that their assumptions might provide an important stimulus to and legitimation of that nuclear policy.

The key point, again, is stable deterrence and the underlying assumption that deterrence is stable. One critic simply didn't believe deterrence can ever be stable. He first said he didn't think the current system of nuclear deterrence was stable, and when pressed by the question 'Do you think it would be a desirable goal if it was stable?' replied,

> ... that's rather like saying 'Do you think a square circle is a good idea?' I don't think it's stable ... because it's a constant struggle of technology to improve and ... because it rests on a threat and ... you're constantly increasing the threat to the other side to respond. So I think it's a dynamic process: it's not of its nature a stable process.

There is no question of the critics agreeing that 'it is 99.95 [per cent] stable' nor of nuclear deterrence working 'for the rest of human history'. As one of them said, 'You can't really believe that for the next thousand years people are going to go on deploying nuclear weapons without using them.'

Perhaps just as striking is the different way of approaching the issue. Whereas the decision-makers rest their arguments on assumptions about individual rationality and focus on what people in possession of nuclear weapons will think and do, the critics take a wider view. There is a sense of people as limited in power, part of a small moment of history, caught up in a vicious circle in which they spin but seem unable to control. Instead of rationality and planning there is paradox and muddle; instead of the cool pursuit of intentional goals there is the escalating inter-reaction of technology and threat. This disagreement hinges, of course, on the vital question of whether or not the system of nuclear deterrence is under control at all.

The moral issue divides the decision-makers and their critics too. Most decision-makers seek to avoid the moral issue by saying that the weapons are for deterrence, not for use. However, the basis for this view was firmly rejected by one nuclear decision-maker:

> The distinction between deterrence and war fighting ... always seems to me as, stripped down, fundamentally bogus. Weapons deter by their capabilities for use when the chips are down and if they have no possibility for use then they can't deter. If deterrence fails ... the Russians look us in the eye and march, then the weapons are there to be used to defend us.

Although he did not go on to consider the moral implications of this view, it is clear that he would believe that any intention to use nuclear weapons is morally acceptable. The critics disagree:

I think the root of my strongest belief is moral ... the deployment of nuclear weapons is undoubtedly immoral from the point of view of conditional intention ... I'm using intention in quite a formal way, not meaning that these particular people who are manufacturing or developing these weapons are saying 'I'm going to use these weapons' ... But I'm saying human beings have to be responsible for their intentions. In that formal sense there's undoubtedly an intention to use these weapons, and it's a present intention. And there's something profoundly immoral in human beings doing that.

This disagreement may owe something to differing perceptions of the weapons themselves. If nuclear weapons are not essentially different from any other kind of weapons, questions about their possession and use can be assimilated into traditions and systems of thought which pre-date the existence of the weapons – in particular the 'just war doctrine'. One decision-maker said, 'I don't think I make as sharp a distinction in my mind between nuclear weapons and others as some people do', and another added, 'I suppose it's a sort of emotive word "nuclear", like that. I can conceive of worse weapons than nuclear – chemical, disease ...' On a rather different tack, but with the same underlying assumption, '... a nuclear conflict which I simply don't believe will ever happen. If it did, I believe it would probably lead to less awful consequences than a conventional conflict ...'

Behind these comments seems to lie a belief that nuclear weapons can be discriminating:

It's nothing to do with people in Minsk and Leningrad ... It isn't a question of destroying millions of people ... it's a question of dictators knowing that we know where they would be ... and they know they would not survive.

This is firmly rejected by the critics:

... a nuclear weapon is not only enormously more destructive than any previous weapons but it is also, of its nature, indiscriminate in that it almost certainly releases material into the atmosphere which is dangerous, lethal, for a long time and which has effects on generations to come ...

Once again, there seems to be a wide as opposed to a narrow focus to these views. None of the decision-makers referred to such long-term effects of the use of nuclear weapons, and the critics referred not just to these but to the long-term effects even of possession of the weapons.

Turning to the threat, the critics agreed that there is no present threat of attack by the Soviet Union. But whereas the decision-makers perceive the threat as a long-term risk of the use of military force against the UK, the critics have a completely different view: 'I don't feel under threat except from the big global threats ...'

Not surprisingly, the decision-makers' thoughts turn to weapons, military strategy and defence policy when they consider threat. Closely linked to this is the assumption that what needs to be defended is 'the territorial and political integrity of a country ...' For the critics, what needs to be defended is something like a way of life which will require the preservation of our natural environment and the elimination of the suffering which would otherwise breed hostile resentment of that way of life.

Finally, we come to a slightly elusive topic – uncertainty. For the decision-makers, British nuclear defence policy seems to rest ultimately on two uncertainties. First, on the uncertainty of relying on the Americans: 'I really do think that the dangers of relying on the American nuclear position is much too great to risk.'

Secondly it rests on a further fundamental uncertainty:

... this is the whole point; that so far as your adversary is concerned he doesn't know whether you would or wouldn't [use nuclear weapons]. But an individual British Prime Minister may have made up his or her mind that in no circumstances would they do that, but having done so then it's his or her duty, if he wants the policy to work, to take every possible step to conceal that.

Stable deterrence then rests on the fact that no-one knows what people would be prepared to do. For the critics, there is no uncertainty:

I know what people are not prepared to do. They're not prepared to blow up their families and the world ... To me, there's no uncertainty, unless we're commanded by lunatics. Britain would never use a nuclear weapon against the Soviet Union ... and so if the Soviets did send their million troops to take the Orkneys there's nothing we would do about it at all. Full stop. Everybody knows that ... and I also know perfectly well there's no uncertainty that America would ... sacrifice a major city for one of our major cities: never. There's no American 'umbrella'.

Again, the nuclear decision-makers and the critics are looking in rather different directions. The decision-makers look at the prevention of intentional nuclear war, and see uncertainty as crucial for keeping the peace. The critics rule out the possibility of an intentional nuclear war and, when asked about uncertainty, think immediately of the difficulties of preventing escalation in the heat of battle, and the risks of accidental nuclear war. Behind this difference in viewpoint lies the most fundamental difference of all. First, a decision-maker: 'If by nuclear war you mean going all the way up to everybody throwing everything – the world is obliterated ... almost anything is preferable to that.'

Now a critic: 'But to me nothing is worth blowing up the world for.'

The critic cannot accept that 'almost anything is preferable to that.'

Conclusions

When they were invented nuclear weapons were designed to be weapons of war. Now, decision-makers believe they are weapons to prevent war by means of stable deterrence. To adapt them to this new purpose has required the acceptance of a whole series of assumptions – for example that they are the best guarantee against aggression, and that possession of them involves no risks of accidental war nor any threat to another nation.

The tension between these new assumptions and the original purpose of the weapons produces some dilemmas. In a serious crisis politicians would have to balance the prior commitment to use nuclear weapons with the need to maintain control and delay irreversible measures. To be faced with such a dilemma seems a curious consequence of a system which is designed to preserve stability. Even the kind of stability which is sought by such a system may be unattainable. An enduring political stability cannot be based on freezing the status quo: it must allow for the resolution of grievances and conflicts by changes to forms of political organisation and ultimately to the boundaries and legitimacy of current nation-states. But while states hold each other under threat with nuclear weapons, it is hard to see how such change could take place. The system of stability, in other words, may be self-defeating.

None of this is meant to suggest that the nuclear decision-makers have not thought long and hard about these issues. Rather it is to suggest that the thinking behind the current production and deployment of nuclear weapons may owe much more to the past, the genesis of the weapons and a view of politics conditioned by the Second World War and its aftermath than it does to the future. If that future is to exist at all we have, at the very least, to be clear which of the assumptions made by nuclear weapons decision-makers are realistic and justified, and which are not.

We have not attempted to make that discrimination: our task has been the prior one of presenting what seem to us to be their assumptions. What would happen if those which were found to be unwarranted were abandoned we cannot say. But to make any unwarranted assumption about nuclear weapons is to take an unacceptable risk.

DISCUSSION

Question: Did the decision-makers you interviewed think that they were controlling technological development, or did they recognise that technology is driving military policy rather than vice-versa?

Scilla Elworthy: We found an almost awestruck reverence for science and technology amongst nuclear decision-makers, and an unquestioning desire to have always the most up-to-date of everything. They thought in terms of a pioneering scientific spirit, of breaking technological barriers, with little questioning as to the goals of science or caution that disadvantages might accompany the advantages. This basic bent obviously feeds into the desire to 'keep ahead' and the conviction that we must. From this follows the negotiate-from-strength assumption (which ignores that if two countries take that position the result is a never-ending nuclear arms race!) That unquestioning trust in technology would be one of the most productive areas to explore in discussions with them.

Dr Frank Barnaby: There's no doubt that it's the momentum of technological development that is driving our military policy. Military planners and politicians are presented with technological *faits accomplis* and have to invent policies and rationales retrospectively. But I think there is also a shadowy group of people in the background who do realise where this military technology is heading, and are encouraging it. They are the people who actually want a nuclear first-strike capability. Curiously, some of these people get so alarmed at what they've seen from the inside, the direction things are going in, that they start to warn the public as soon as they retire. But they never do this before they retire !

Scilla Elworthy: That is why General Schmähling, head of West Germany's military think-tank, is so remarkable. He is a senior serving officer who has broken ranks to reveal the danger of what is going on, and how he disagrees with it. This was widely reported in December 1988 and affected many people. He told me that he came to his present point of view (opposition to any theatre nuclear weapons in Europe) when he began to ask questions as to what really would happen in the event of a 'small' nuclear weapon being used. He was so alarmed by the lack of serious response to this that he decided 'flexible response' was a dangerous policy. I believe he's been quite severely disciplined.

Note

This research was funded by Barrow and Geraldine S Cadbury Trust. Serious scholars wishing to check the accuracy and balance of the quotations we have used may have access to the interview material, in some cases under conditions which will preserve the anonymity of the decision-makers and the confidentiality of the interview.

8

Children's Views – Talking with Young Children About Nuclear Issues

RUTH DAVIES and LYNN BARNETT

Introduction

When members of SPINA began to meet in 1987, it became apparent that an area of concern for many members was how children and young people think and feel about living in a world of nuclear weapons. What part does the threat of nuclear war play in the minds of children? How does this threat relate to other political issues (domestic, international or environmental), as well as their immediate emotional environments? In considering these questions it was noted that an increasing body of research,[89] principally from abroad, indicates a widespread and serious concern among various groups of young people. While there is not a great deal of such work on children in Britain, what has been carried out[17,38] points to a similar experience for young people here.

A MORI poll in conjunction with the *Independent*[72] surveyed 1,252 of 'Thatcher's children', including a special sample of 600 aged 15–28 years. A question asking which two or three things caused most worry revealed AIDS and nuclear war as the most worrying. While older people were more worried about drug addiction and the environment, young women were 'substantially more frightened than young men of nuclear war'; this has been found in other surveys.

Helen Haste,[50] studying British young people aged 11–14 years, found four issues created the greatest anxiety. In order of concern, they were: unemployment, war, death and AIDS.

Goldenring and Doctor[44] state that using 'the most scientifically designed sample yet' on thousands of young people in the USA and USSR they found that 'there can now be no reasonable doubt that worry about the nuclear threat is significant for a large proportion of young people and this concern crosses all racial, economic and religious groupings in developed nations worldwide.'

In discussing this work two points began to emerge: first, that the emphasis had hitherto been on adolescent populations, with little attention to what had preceded the worries expressed by teenagers. Secondly, the methodology of existing research had relied on large-scale surveys with questionnaires. While this served to establish that there was a problem to be investigated, it told us little about how individual children were thinking, whether they perceived a threat from nuclear weapons and, if so, how they coped with it.

It was decided therefore to concentrate on children under ten years of age, and to explore with them their perceptions of nuclear weapons, using an interview style that would be open-ended and allow some depth of investigation. The initial task would be for each member of the study group to talk with a small number of children to see what themes and issues emerged, and what techniques were most useful in talking to children of this age group. The results of these initial interviews are presented here.

Methodology

Part of the purpose of this pilot study was to explore and experiment with methodology, but certain principles were agreed upon from the start. There was no formal interview schedule, so that although the interviewers had certain questions in mind they were free to follow the child's direction as much as possible. The children were asked if they ever heard anything on the news that worried them, then if they had ever heard anything about nuclear weapons. They were asked when and how they had heard about nuclear weapons, and how they felt about them. If they were worried, how did they cope with the worry? Did they discuss these things in the family, with friends, or at school? One area of questioning examined what children felt could be done, either by themselves or others about nuclear weapons. Also they were asked what they thought their parents felt about these matters, and how they dealt with them. Some of the interviews used visual material as a stimulus, and asked children to draw what had been discussed and talk about their drawings. The interviewers refrained from expressing their own opinions or commenting on the children's opinions. Neither did interviewers discuss with children the accuracy of what they said, for example factual errors made by the children were not corrected. Children were interviewed singly, in pairs and in one case in a group, where possible in private and not in the company of parents. Interviews were recorded either by cassette or video tape. No attempt was made to select a representative sample. The children were either known personally to the interviewers or their colleagues, or had parents contacted by word-of-mouth. The aim of the pilot study was not to establish generalities about children's thinking, but rather to examine in detail how individual children thought.

The youngest child was five years old and the oldest nine. There were nine boys and six girls. The interviews were carried out between January 1987 and September 1988, most during the summer of 1988.

What the Children Said

Images and Associations with Nuclear War

Figure 8.1 presents some of the ideas the children had, and possible relationships between them. It was clear that none of the children had a very distinct, discrete concept of 'nuclear war' or 'the Bomb', even when they were in fact quite knowledgeable and articulate on these subjects. Two important areas were closely related and often mentioned as if they were the same thing: nuclear power and warfare in general. A second important factor was that, for some children at least, raising the question of nuclear war brought up fears or worries of a more personal nature, to do with death or aggression in their immediate experience, whether in reality or fantasy.

Figure 8.1 Children's Images and Associations with Nuclear War

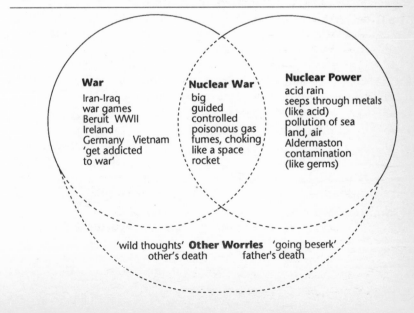

War
Iran-Iraq
war games
Beruit WWII
Ireland
Germany Vietnam
'get addicted
to war'

Nuclear War
big
guided
controlled
poisonous gas
fumes, choking
like a space
rocket

Nuclear Power
acid rain
seeps through metals
(like acid)
pollution of sea
land, air
Aldermaston
contamination
(like germs)

'wild thoughts' **Other Worries** 'going beserk'
other's death   father's death

To begin with the concept of nuclear war, many of the children's images were very concrete ones to do with how a nuclear weapon works and what it does. A very common idea, that nuclear weapons are immensely powerful, was expressed by saying that a single bomb could destroy 'the whole of Britain' or 'all of London'. One boy accounted for this immense power by explaining that a nuclear weapon was like 'a bit of the sun'. Nuclear weapons were also considered special because they were in some sense more controlled, they could be fired and guided automatically, for example. Concerning the delivery, a common visual image was that a nuclear weapon was like a space rocket. Most of the children had an idea that there was something else which made nuclear weapons different. This was explained as being like poisonous gas fumes, which would kill people by choking them or poisoning them. This is possibly a reference to radiation; like a gas, radiation is invisible.

The concept of radiation was commonly mentioned in connection with nuclear power, and may be the vital link between the two groups of images. Some children, in particular those who seemed to be most knowledgeable, lumped together 'nuclear things', possibly because the adults they knew who were active in anti-nuclear movements did the same. Some very vivid and frightening imagery came up here. Radiation, seen as the chief hazard of nuclear power, is pervasive, it seeps through most substances, even strong ones like metals. In this sense, it is similar to another dangerous substance, acid. Indeed acid rain was mentioned as one of the consequences of nuclear power. Another powerful image connected with radiation was its contaminating quality, it could get into your food, or on your hands, and so into your body. Nuclear power was admitted to be a source of electricity by one boy, but was also a source of pollution. Most of the children had heard of the accident at Chernobyl, but often felt that it was sufficiently distant not to endanger them personally. The idea that things were happening 'a long way away' was a comforting thought for many of the children. Even though they said a nuclear accident or explosion would be immensely powerful, they also said that only if it happened on or near their house would they be in personal danger. One child who lived close to a nuclear power station and was clearly worried about it, felt able to remain safe, for example by avoiding swimming in the sea.

A third topic discussed by the children was warfare in general. Several current or recent conflicts were mentioned, such as

Vietnam, Iran–Iraq, South Africa and Beirut. Some of the children believed that nuclear weapons were, or might be, used in these wars. On the other hand many children's concepts of modern warfare were anachronistic, one child even maintaining that modern wars were fought with swords and shields. This was commonest amongst the younger children. Amongst the older children the Second World War was a common source of ideas and images, probably as a result of TV, comics and school history lessons. Apparently as a result of this several children believed Germany to be a potential or actual enemy of Britain. Some children talked about war games and how these were regarded by adults. There was a feeling that such play was disapproved of, because it could lead to an acceptance of war or even because children 'might get addicted to war'. While this may indeed represent the opinion of some teachers and parents, it is also possible that the children themselves sometimes feel uncomfortable about this sort of play. In fact several children stated that they refused to take part in war games and had arguments with friends over this. Despite this general disapproval of war and fighting it was noticeable that the drawings produced by the children, especially the boys, showed war as an exciting and eventful situation. They did not attempt to portray peace as an active process. One boy secretly did a cartoon of a man shouting 'War is fun' on the back of his drawing of peace, which he had discussed with the interviewer.

Feelings

Nearly all the children interviewed expressed fairly strong feelings in reaction to the topic, whether this was simply discussed or presented in pictures. It was obvious in some cases that what they felt could not be expressed by them in words, but was clear in their voices, gestures and drawings. Certainly for some the pictures stimulated responses where words alone did not, and one girl actually commented that while pictures made her feel things, just talking didn't. One boy drew a picture which seemed to express strong feelings of being attacked or endangered that did not come out in his talk; the picture showed a boy swimming in a dangerously polluted sea, surrounded by dead fish, with an aeroplane dropping bombs directly onto him. The commonest emotions expressed were sadness, fear, and occasionally hostility. Some children said that they would feel afraid if these things were happening near them or to them, but felt sufficiently distanced not to experience fear directly. The younger children expressed strongest fears relating to their immediate family and home while the older ones tended to show strong empathy with people caught up in wars at the moment, and this served as the basis for their opposition to war. Some children had bad dreams, even for one girl so bad that 'you wake up sweating.' For some children, the topic of nuclear war aroused strong anxiety, perhaps to do with their own aggressive feelings. One boy talked about 'wild thoughts' that could make you go 'all funny in the head and start doing things very dangerous'. In the group discussion, when the children drew a picture together, one boy commented several times 'everything's going berserk.'[V2]

Coping

How do children cope with these strong and frightening feelings? One option already mentioned is, in imagination, physically to distance themselves from the things that are frightening. This works even for children who emphasise the widespread and pervasive effects of nuclear weapons or nuclear accidents. For example, one child thought that pollution from Chernobyl could drift a long way in clouds blown by winds, but didn't think they could be blown as far as Britain. Since it would be difficult to have gained that much information about the Chernobyl accident without also learning of the effects on Britain, this suggests some suppression of the really scary information. Sometimes this would assume a fantastical aspect, as in the group discussion where the children talked about escaping to the moon with bags of oxygen. Other children coped by avoiding the subject and indeed they did this during the interview. A more conscious method mentioned by several children is to distract oneself by thinking about something else, something nice instead. One boy who adopted this approach also said that he had got used to the fear, whereas previously he had suffered with nightmares. Another strategy is to believe that things will or might improve. Children had several grounds for optimism. One was that nobody would really want a nuclear war, because of the destruction and suffering it would cause. Related to this, some children knew something about the INF Treaty and saw this as at least a good start. Finally, some children believed that nuclear weapons could be got rid of if there were sufficient public pressure for this and made suggestions as to how this would happen. On the other hand, some children believed there was nothing at all that ordinary people, themselves or their parents, could do to influence matters. Only people with special power or responsibility could change things, and one boy suggested he might join the army and then sabotage nuclear weapons. The question of who can or should do something about the possibility of nuclear war will be considered next.

Responsibility

The children were asked what, if anything, ordinary people could do about the threat of nuclear war and how this might be achieved. While some children believed there was nothing that could be done, many suggestions were offered. In most cases, children believed that change could only be effected indirectly by ordinary people, who would have to influence those in power. Margaret Thatcher and Ronald Reagan were named as people who could do something if they chose, or were persuaded. Some children thought that Thatcher or Reagan would then have to pressurise the armed forces or the anonymous people who have the bombs in order to make them give them up. The children had lots of ideas about how to influence politicians. Some relied on conventional electoral politics, such as electing a (Labour) government who would disarm. Others talked about the usual methods of pressure groups, making posters, having demonstrations and so on. These were seen as activities they could take part in themselves, and in fact some of the children had been involved in this way. Writing to the Prime Minister was mentioned; one girl had a friend who had done this only to receive a patronising reply, from which she concluded that you would have to organise lots of people to do it together. Some of the younger children believed that nuclear weapons could be disposed of by giving money. This is perhaps an analogy with other worthy causes to which children are invited to contribute. The money would be used to give to the bad people who want to fight wars, so that they would stop. While children themselves could help with this it would be more the responsibility of rich people to give. Rich people mentioned were Margaret Thatcher and the Queen. Finally one child talked about the classic technique of nonviolence: appealing directly to individuals involved in nuclear arms or nuclear power, to make them 'give up on it'.

Adults

The children were asked what they thought their parents and teachers felt about these matters and whether they were discussed with them. All the children believed that their parents knew about nuclear weapons, not surprisingly. Most thought that their parents were themselves worried about nuclear war, as were their older siblings. Yet the children were told not to worry. Sometimes, they felt, their parents were worrying about it but not saying anything. It seemed clear that the children were well aware of adult anxieties and also in most cases that they, the children, were not 'supposed to know'. They were often protecting the adults close to them by not raising the topic they sensed was taboo. If they felt their parents were worried several of the children said they tried to distract their parents, comfort them or cheer them up. Clearly this is a heavy responsibility for a child to bear, especially when the subject of nuclear war is felt to be unmentionable. Those children whose parents did talk openly about the threat of nuclear war recognised that they were unusual. One boy in this position thought that adults in general would be very surprised if they knew how much children worried about nuclear issues. Although it is an upsetting topic it should not be avoided, most children felt, because it is so important to understand, and perhaps to take some action. There is no point, one child said, in avoiding the topic so as not to upset children, as they are already upset.

Schools, it appears, are also evading the issue. A few children thought that perhaps in secondary schools there might be some discussion of the issue, but no child had had any teaching on the subject in school so far. Various explanations were offered for this omission. Some children recognised that, for some reason, the issue was a sensitive one for teachers. This was expressed as its being 'rude'. One boy thought that it was a case of political manipulation: his headteacher approved of nuclear weapons and so his class teacher would not dare teach about them for fear of dismissal. A more sophisticated explanation offered by several children was that schools were reluctant to raise the subject because children might conclude that nuclear weapons or warfare in general were good things. There was a danger that children could 'get addicted to war'. In this case they might grow up to join the armed forces. Of course, some children felt that the opposite was more likely: if schools taught about nuclear war, children would be against it.

A general conclusion that can be drawn from what these children said is that they feel adults avoid the topic of nuclear war. This does not help them since they are worried anyway and they would welcome the chance to talk about it.

Comparison of Results with Other Studies

The findings of our pilot project are similar to the few other studies of this age group.

Greenwald and Zeitlin,[45] two American family therapists, found in a group of 23 children aged 6–12 years that 'the nuclear issue is definitely a strong concern among these children.' All had a basic understanding of the nuclear bomb and its power – the younger children tending to under- or overestimate the degree of power, the older ones being more realistic.

They also found that this age-group of children had various ways of dealing with the nuclear threat, which can be summarised briefly as:

1. That war could be avoided before it happens by making people vote to get rid of weapons; by telling them how dangerous and powerful nuclear weapons are; by writing letters to powerful people.
2. Latency-age boys cope by thinking of technological solutions, for example alien spaceships/weapons, as the current study has also found.
3. Many children have escape fantasies, for example going to live on the moon, as also in this study's group discussion.
4. Children struggling at this age (6–12 years) to develop a sense of fairness say 'it [nuclear war] is not fair.' They are trying to develop a sense of control and confidence in relation to violence yet at the same time they see governments indulging in it. Children see a dilemma in appealing to the very people who are creating the problem to stop it.
5. They do not discuss the subject amongst peers, but do feel it should be talked about in school.
6. They often don't talk about nuclear issues to parents because they want to be reassured by their parents but fear their parents might feel helpless too and therefore don't raise it, for the sake of both parents and themselves. Also, they cannot bear to feel they have impotent parents and want to protect their parents from feeling 'bad'.
7. Common in 9–12 year-olds is a fear of chaos, of things falling apart. Six out of 23 of Greenwald and Zeitlin's sample had bad nightmares about nuclear matters. For children 'the scariest image is separation: of not being able to find their parents.' Children aged 5–8 years describe effects in concrete personal terms.
8. The younger children have outdated ideas about war and weapons.
9. Sources of knowledge are mainly television and films.

10. Concepts of peace are less well developed than concepts of war. Peace tended to be viewed as a rather negative state involving inactivity and passivity – hence a state of mind as implied by the phrase 'peace of mind' rather than a positive good which could be actively worked for.

The Scottish psychiatrist Jim Dyer[23] suggests that there is a need for more investigation of the interactions amongst knowledge, feelings and attitudes of young people, and the link between these and 'family environment variables'. For example studies of children in other stress situations show the strong protective effect of a united family (see similar comments by Tizard below).

Dyer cites Jones and Sanders[55] and Davies[18] who asked children if they want more teaching about nuclear issues in school. A majority said they did, as in our sample. Dyer concludes, 'There is no evidence that a nuclear threat produces actual psychiatric disorders in children' but adds that this cannot be entirely discounted until there has been more study.

Several writers feel that the nuclear threat has affected children and young people developmentally. John Mack,[63] an American analyst, queried its effect on the development of impulse control, capacity to delay gratification, ability to form long-term ideals and relationships, and the development of a sense of social responsibility. Reporting her 1988 study of New Zealand schoolchildren, Pam Oliver[73] showed that increased optimism about the future followed that country's nuclear-free policy.

Greenwald and Zeitlin[45] suggest that the nuclear threat has affected people in all the various life-stages (as delineated by Erikson[28]). They suggest that in each stage of life people are now limited in their ability to complete the relevant developmental tasks, because the process of engaging with other generations and the culture at large has been restricted, in the following ways:

School Age and Latency

During this stage the major task is to develop a sense of industry, an ability to be active and exploratory, and to overcome feelings of powerlessness and inferiority by developing skills and a sense of capability and confidence. Much of this is based on identifying with adults who, if they do not themselves feel capable or confident (as few do in relation to nuclear weapons), are not particularly good models. Is it any wonder that children of this age turn to Superman, star-beings and other unrealistically powerful nonhuman models? Significantly, the Canadian researcher Susan Gold-berg,[41] and others, have found that children of parents who are actively involved in the peace movement feel more anxious but also more able to cope and be active themselves.

Another model for dealing with feelings of powerlessness and inferiority is developing a sense of false capability. (It is surely upon this model that such notions as nuclear deterrence and Star-Wars are based.)

Adolescence

The tasks of this stage are to consolidate identity (by integrating the sexual and aggressive drives) and to make commitments. Again, what are the role-models for this? How can adolescents make commitments if they believe the future is uncertain, which, as we know from various studies, a large majority do believe.

Adulthood

Greenwald and Zeitlin[45] suggest that in this stage generativity is threatened. How can one have children and how can a future generation be guided and new ideas discovered if there may well be no future?

Old Age

To feel one can die well, with a good life spent well, one must feel that the things one has worked for and believed in will continue. To whom can one pass all one's values and culture if, for example, nuclear conflict results in the 'nuclear winter' which changes the basis of any surviving society beyond recognition?

On the other hand, the psychoanalyst Henri Parens,[74] contrasting his findings with those of non-analysts, states that in his 20 years of analytic work with children and adolescents there have been 'surprisingly few associations to and dreams of this danger and, hence, little evidence of anxiety arising directly from the threat of nuclear war'. This finding, he says, is consistent with that of colleagues with whom he has discussed this issue. Hanna Segal[85] suggests, however, that this is because the analytic tech-nique employed by these American analysts does not address early 'psychotic' mental states, unlike the Kleinian technique. She main-tains that all her (adult) patients have mentioned the 'primitive terror' associated with nuclear weapons.

Parens gives another explanation. He uses the concept of 'sali-ence' (as does Barbara Tizard[94]) suggesting that the nuclear threat is 'experience-distant' in the clinical context of experience and object relationships which make up his analytic sessions. He also says that it may not be relevant to his patients in relation to the symptoms for which they sought his treatment. Parens suggests alternatively (as does Segal in Chapter 4) that the lack of mention of the nuclear threat by his young patients may be linked with the erection of 'powerful defences' against the awareness of vulnerability and help-lessness.

He considers that the capacity for direct experiencing of the threat of nuclear disaster only emerges at puberty with the giving up of the parents' centrality, the development of a capacity for abstract thought, the experiencing of the new separate self as vulnerable to threat or danger and the expanding awareness of community and world issues. Parens also claims that much of his analysis is concerned with the pre-latency years of his patients (that is, before six years of age) and their drives, when they are not in touch with the nuclear issue. In contrast, Segal considers that nuclear terror is derived from very early fears of psychically falling apart.

Escalona[29] and Friedman[37] claim that awareness of the nuclear threat may begin to be represented internally from four or five years old. But what it actually means to children of this age is another matter, particularly as they cannot fully grasp the inevita-bility of death until early adolescence. Parens claims that pre-latency children are aware of danger mainly in relation to the family context – their most prominent fears are of object-loss, loss of love and of valued body-parts. To them danger, as we also found in this pilot study, concerns losing their parents, and nuclear danger is only known secondarily through the care-givers' either conscious or unconscious anxiety. And it is immediacy which is important to young children – we found they mentioned recent happenings such as aeroplane highjacking when talking of things in the news which may have disturbed them.

Anyone who deals with latency-age children knows that they (especially boys) have a great interest in war, with elaborate fanta-sies, games, drawings and play. This is related to the central task of this age which is learning self-control of impulses and coping with separation from parents while entering the world of their peers.

Boys of this age are struggling with conflict around narcissistic exhibitionism and associated dangers: nuclear weapons serve these ends well, both in power and shape! From a recent study of Dutch children aged 6–12 years involving discussions and over 200 draw-ings of war and peace, Lennaert Vriens (personal communication) found that girls do not like war or drawing war while boys, particularly 8–11 year olds, 'love it'. This parallels our findings.

Parens concludes that amongst young children the nuclear threat, as with any threat, will mobilise anxiety according to the degree to which it is experienced as 'experience-near', and in terms of individual neurotic and characterological make-up. He states that those with obsessional thoughts, hysterical reactivity and phobic tendencies are more likely to attach the nuclear threat to their intrapsychic conflicts.

Barbara Tizard[94] discusses how until recently most research on children and the nuclear threat was carried out with a clinical focus using a medical model: exposure to threat disturbs mental health. But, she says, 'recently new issues and paradigms have been examined.' She feels the medical model has proved unsatisfactory because it cannot account for the following findings: that women and girls express more worry than men; that young women 'are substantially more frightened by nuclear war than men; younger adolescents worry more than older ones; [and there is a] variation in levels of anxiety in different countries and within one country from year to year'. Thus, 'this [medical] model can't explain the effect of the social context nor the role of cognitive factors including beliefs, attitudes and values in mediating the individual's response to the nuclear threat.'

The second model is one concerned with 'coping strategies' which stress cognitive processes (see for example Hamilton *et al.*[48] and Haste[51]). This sees anti-nuclear activism as a style of coping which depends on a particular combination of cognitive and affective elements, whether in adolescents or adults.

A third paradigm discerned by Tizard is the 'context-paradigm'. An example of this is provided by Solantaus[89] who uses Vygotskian theory to show how different families and peers influenced two adolescent girls to change in their reactions to anti-nuclear anxieties; in other words, she considers the interaction of values and beliefs within a social context, looking in detail at individuals.

Thus when studying research on the effects of the nuclear threat on children and adolescents one must be clear what paradigm or model, and what age, family and social context is involved. Those who wish to use research based on the medical model for propaganda reasons will be disappointed, for it is certainly not clear from available results that children under 10 years, still involved in a family context, have reacted with psychiatric disorders to the nuclear threat. But that they do know a lot about it and are concerned about it, especially in relation to their own aggression, is clear, as is their need and desire to talk about it.

Thoughts for Parents and Teachers on Talking with Children about Nuclear War and Related Topics

These children were very clear in their wish that adults would stop avoiding the topic of nuclear war. Yet many adults feel unsure of how to approach these issues, which are, after all, difficult for all of us. It may help to acknowledge firstly that children are not 'innocent' about nuclear weapons; they learn about them very early and cannot be protected from knowing, however much this might be wished. The points that follow relate specifically to discussing nuclear issues with children, but may also be relevant, for example, to environmental issues. Teachers and parents should bear in mind, however, that during the interviews some children were reminded of unpleasant feelings that were not related, for example grief at a recent bereavement. This possibility should be kept in mind.

The fact that children are already worried about nuclear war does not mean, however, that we should not be very careful in how we talk with children. It is important for adults undertaking this task to be fully aware of their own feelings on the subject. The prospect of a nuclear war, especially in regard to children, will naturally arouse very deep and strong feelings in adults. Unless these have been fully explored and acknowledged, it would be difficult to separate one's own emotional needs and responses from the child's. Although it is important for adults to admit to children that they too feel afraid, or angry, children should not be burdened with the full force of these feelings from adults on whom they depend. Young children rely on adults (their parents and, collectively, adult society) to make the world a safe place for them, and while we may sometimes feel this is not possible, this might be too frightening for children.

Sometimes it may seem difficult to give children the chance to talk about nuclear issues in an open and informal way. One method that might be useful is to use news stories as a starting point. It was clear in the interviews reported here that current and recent news stories were prominent in children's minds. Parents can talk with children while they watch the news, or teachers can start the day by talking about what the children have been hearing and seeing on the news media. This can work well even with very young children. It is important to ask children how they feel about what they have heard, and not just to ask them what they think or understand. Doing drawings and paintings can be helpful if they are talked about too.

It is also important to gauge what we tell children according to their needs, understanding and level of development. In this respect there can be no substitute for knowing a child really well. It can help, however, to be very sensitive to what a child is actually saying and to respond to the question that was asked rather than the one you think might or should have been asked. Thus, detailed descriptions of the results of a nuclear explosion, which would indeed be very distressing, are unlikely to be necessary. Although some of the children interviewed said they would like to know more about nuclear weapons, the opportunity should always be offered to explore how they feel as well. On the subject of factual information, it should be remembered that children often misunderstand the things they hear from adult conversations or news media and these misunderstandings may be a cause of distress. For example many children believed that Britain and Germany were enemies and might possibly go to war. Such a misunderstanding can be simply and honestly dealt with. As well as giving children the chance to learn about nuclear weapons and explore their feelings about them, most adults will be anxious to help children find ways of coping with ideas that are profoundly distressing. While some children simply denied any uncomfortable feelings, most of the children interviewed for this pilot study had more active solutions which fall into two main groups. Firstly there were children who coped with fear by distracting themselves. They would think about something else, something nice, and so the fear was replaced by good feelings. It may be that this would only work for children who have sufficient confidence that the adult world will eventually find solutions. The second approach was to do something about the problem and children had many ideas about what kinds of things they could do. This seems a very positive approach, which adults can support children in. It might help to talk about things that other children have done, for example the letter writing campaign organised by children in the United States. It may be that the methods children suggest seem naively optimistic to an adult observer, but the important thing is that they are taking an active part in solving a problem which troubles them.[V3]

To conclude, it seems clear that most adults' practice of avoiding the topic of nuclear issues with children, whatever the motivation, is seen by children as failing them. Although it is commonly held that young children have little interest in such matters, and could not understand them in any case, the evidence shows that they are aware and concerned. Adults should not leave them to bear this knowledge alone. The responsibility of researchers is to explore what are the most helpful ways of sharing with children, and allowing them to find their own ways of coping.

Part III
Directions of Change

9

Military Pomp and Nuclear Circumstance

ALASTAIR MACKIE

'I don't know what effect these men will have upon the enemy but by God they frighten me' said either King George III or the Duke of Wellington. They were referring to a weapons system, well known to medicine, described as having two legs, headache, backache, homesickness and blisters. The Duke, top of the top brass of the day, was just about to snatch victory from the jaws of defeat. Today's top brass, in contrast, are just about to snatch defeat from the jaws of victory. The enemy in 1815 was a French megalomaniac. Today it's a universal megalomaniac epitomised as the Bomb. It might help our deliberations on the nuclear mentality in relation to dynamics and change to consider the opposite: stasis, resistance to change, immutability in its military aspect.

That impending defeat doesn't have to happen. One way of explaining how it might be avoided is through another lot of brass – the Soviet military. Ever since the first Czar came to power in 1547 they have ensured that armed might has taken precedence over every other aspiration because of the invasions that began with Genghis Khan 300 years before and have continued since then. The invasion psychosis these invasions caused got a great boost in 1917 when a Western coalition tried to sabotage the Soviet Revolution by invading; and another in 1941 when the Nazis killed 20 million Russians and caused damage whose effects still persist. This invasion psychosis also underlay the brandishing by the USSR against Western Europe of the enormous forces they assembled to throw out the Germans. It was the source of the long series of outrages from the Berlin blockade to the epic folly of Afghanistan. It was the Soviet High Command's excuse for assuming that the nuclear devastation of Russia plus an American invasion of the homeland across the bridgehead of Europe were strategic inevitabilities. Fascinatingly, that's changed: this is no longer a Soviet strategic assumption, only a contingency. According to the leading Western Sovietologist Professor McGwire[66] of the Brookings Institution, that change led the Soviet military to acquiesce in the

107

unilateral test ban moratorium. Then, after the blunder of the routine replacement of the SS4 and 5 with the SS20 in Europe, it led to a sequence of encouraging actions: the nuclear-free world initiative, Reykjavik, INF and Gorbachev's current offers and undertakings about weapon cuts. It was the change of circumstances in the Middle East that allowed this to happen: Islam, Israel, President Carter's use of the Gulf to get himself elected, and the freebooting of the US Sixth Fleet against Libya to get rid of Syrian-based terrorists, all led the Soviets to see the Middle East, not Europe, as the main risk area. They changed their force dispositions and command structure accordingly. The military changes were welcomed by their political colleagues trying, as Gorbachev still is, to deal with internal Islamic troubles, turbulence in the republics, racial upsets and economic prostration. None of that means Soviet generals have suddenly become angelic or even compliant. Very much still in being is the Soviet Bomb, despite SALT, test embargoes, the end of weapons-grade plutonium and even the prospective 50 per cent cut in strategic nuclear forces.

When we consider Western responses to that Soviet change it is, oddly, much harder to distinguish military from political policy in NATO and the USA than in the Soviet Union and Warsaw Pact! But we do know that there have been American military pressures from the earliest days of the Bomb to use it pre-emptively against the Soviet Union, whose surveillance must have detected those pressures long before they were known generally. This must have informed the Soviet expectation of inevitable nuclear war and Western intentions. As that change of Soviet emphasis from Europe to the Middle East was happening, contemporary changes in NATO, at the instance of the US Joint Chiefs of Staff, were very different. Reagan's Defence Secretary Caspar Weinberger, who never could stand up to the generals, horrified some at least of the Allies by trying to cast NATO in a world role.[98] The US Air Force turned a drone aircraft conceived as a decoy into what we now know as the Cruise missile. And the Soviet SS20 was used as a pretext against which to deploy Cruise and Pershing. Not to be outdone, the US Navy under Secretary Lehman, who never could stand up to the admirals, became the 600-ship, 15 carrier-group force it now is (a carrier group, if centred on London, would stretch to central Poland and northern Italy). The US Congress Armed Services Committee was told at the time that the US Navy's new war role had been extended from escorting reinforcement convoys across the Atlantic to nothing less than carrying out carrier-based nuclear air-strikes against the USSR and assault landings by the Marines in north west Russia.[97] Most important of all, within 'the first five minutes of war' would be the destruction by hunter-killer submarines of Soviet missile-carrying submarines forming the Soviet last-ditch, second-strike capability. The effect of that New Maritime Strategy and especially the submarines' destruction is to ensure that war will not only become nuclear but terminally obliterative at once. The US Army similarly transformed its land strategy over the same period. To the classic containment of the invading hordes which had sustained the NATO armies for decades there has been added a great offensive capability. This new US Army AirLand Battle concept is the nuclear descendant of the Nazi blitzkrieg. A variant is NATO's Follow On Force Attack which involves a deep strike into Warsaw Pact territory, with the first use of nuclear weapons. This is confirmed by US Congressional testimony[96] and the one prestigious British military journal[14] – in flat refutation of British government assurances in both Houses of Parliament about first use of nuclear weapons.

There is no question, therefore, of balancing forces with the Soviets. Instead, Western reliance on nuclear forces is increased and any possibility of conflict remaining non-nuclear or limited-nuclear is reduced.

Another form of NATO response consists of the military encouraging politicians to resist and obstruct any arms control or slowing of the arms race. The US and British answer to 18 months of no Soviet testing was to keep testing new weapons. At Reykjavik it was a matter of preventing President Reagan matching his fine words with deeds. The prospect of the INF Treaty gave NATO's then Supreme Commander General Bernard Rogers what he inelegantly described as 'gas pains'. His successor General Galvin couldn't resist observing in an unguarded moment that INF brought the chances of war closer. But the reason why INF got through the NATO top brass was that Cruise and Pershing were political, not military, weapons. Their loss will create no gap in the nuclear spectrum, but has increased military pressures to replace them with air- and sea-based Cruise missiles so that NATO will have, after INF, two to three times as many Cruise missiles as INF has eliminated.

Of all the daunting negatives and evasions in response to Soviet disarmament offerings and undertakings, the most fatuous is Mrs Thatcher's gladiatorial exhortation that we British must keep up our guard; even if this consists of the entire British military establishment, it would be much less than the land forces (500,000 in number) that Gorbachev has committed the Soviet Army to demobilising.

As to the future, there is careful provision to ensure that nothing actually happens: no negotiations by NATO about nuclear weapons until there is agreement over non-nuclear weapons, because running the two in parallel would expose the fallacy of balance; no negotiations on NATO and Warsaw Pact armaments as a whole, only on land- and some air-forces, because bringing in naval and the other air-forces would expose the myth of Warsaw Pact superiority; and no looking beyond the numbers at the policies – NATO's offensive strategies and developing first-use capability. The only agreement being allowed any life is START (the Strategic Arms Reduction Talks) though even that is blocked currently; supposedly START demonstrates NATO's good intentions, and even its improbable aim of 50 per cent cuts will leave both sides with the ability to obliterate every city in the world an absurd number of times.

So the Bomb goes on winning. Despite the genuine disarmament initiatives from the USSR, and the West's depressing response of increasing its capacity to wage nuclear war, both Superpowers remain dependants of the Bomb. Soviet initiatives, welcome as they are, have barely touched their nuclear arsenals. Meanwhile Western political and military establishments seek a problem for every solution, and new monsters to continue justifying their existence – nonplussed by the new non-threatening threat from President Gorbachev. To understand why this is, we need first to examine the justifications which the military would put forward, and I will restrict this to the British military establishment.

It would be claimed that politicians make the final decisions, but in fact it is truer to say that military and politicians interact. Soldiers advise and politicians direct on the basis of that advice. That is an excellent way of ensuring that nothing changes, and the old certainties are preserved. And when there is any disagreement it is the military who then carry the day.

Alternatively, it might be said that this continuing nuclear dependency, and any alarming current developments, are not Britain's fault: it's the Superpowers' responsibility; with our very small nuclear forces we barely count in the decision-making. Indeed, we are no more than a small off-shore island of the European mainland. Our great strategic advantage would be our total unimportance were it not for the role which we have arrogated to ourselves as an American advance base and the possessor of what can be passed off as a British Bomb. But this insignificance has never deterred our military. We, the official argument also runs, got NATO off the ground when, with the French, we succeeded in keeping the Germans down and the Americans in Europe. That in itself entitled us to a voice in the councils of the great. We still had an empire, we'd won the war, we'd invented the Bomb, we were on the Security Council; if there's anything the British contribution to NATO strategy lacks, it isn't false modesty. So that excuse won't do either.

Nor again will another excuse rather like it – that formulating strategy is the privilege of the chosen few at the top. That is not so because the top few are preoccupied fighting each other and the civil servants for money and influence. The science and art of strategy is actually practised in the upper middle ranks, by junior generals. The answer lies elsewhere – in the military mind.

The current depressing spectacle of the West continuing to increase its nuclear capacity in the face of real opportunities for disarmament is a consequence of the rigidity and resistance to change of the military mind. Although the military, being people, are a diversity, they have distinctive shared characteristics. The best known is discipline, manifest for most of us in the tribal ritual of the Trooping of the Colour and heel-clicking and saluting. It doesn't end there. It's the only known way of making a man stick a bayonet in the guts of another, drive a frigate at full speed through a sea of drowning people, or hold a bomber steady and deliver its load while it's disintegrating and someone's dying noisily in the back.

Another obvious military characteristic is uniformity – not just dressing in the same clothes but pivoted on a common identity from which some individuals radiate outwards a little, but few very much. It goes back to the time when illiterate peasant boys were dragged from the fields and clustered round epicentral common identities – the signs ancestral to regimental badges. Uniformity's age and indestructibility still show in the deliberately affected speech cultivated by generations of guards and cavalry officers. The military system feeds on it and feeds it. Not for nothing do the soldiers call newly minted subalterns emerging from Sandhurst 'Ruperts'. The product of those military properties is hierarchy. Everything is handed down. Of those who hand it down Britain has more than enough: 584 serving generals and their navy and air-force equivalents. This is far more than most comparable nations; one for every regiment, major ship and squadron, plus countless hundreds of the retired. Almost universally, discipline, uniformity, conformity and hierarchy rule. Apart from an Admiral of the Fleet now deceased, a Field Marshal, two Generals, a Major General, a Brigadier and an Air Commodore – me – none has publicly opposed our nuclear defence policy. In contrast the rest of NATO, the Warsaw Pact, India, Central America and the USA all have groups of senior military dissenters. That doesn't mean there's no British dissent; there are certainly closet British critics. But why so many closed minds? First, because open ones have to be very strong. Almost from the start young officers are thoughtfully furnished with ready-dug intellectual channels, and they're kept shallow. Prince Edward's departure from Royal Marine training some years ago had nothing to do with the lack of fibre – I believe it had everything to do with the removal then from regular officer training of more of its already very slight intellectual content.

The more senior one goes the more devoted to the system one becomes – perhaps out of grateful wonderment that one has been not only tolerated but elevated. That's what gives the military their caryatid property an ever closer and blinder cleavage to 'my service', and in the soldier's case 'my regiment', 'right or wrong'.

There are other, less honourable answers to this question: intellectual confinement's one thing, but intellectual dishonesty's another. 'My service right or wrong' can and does degenerate into more and better for the RAF, for instance, and to hell both with the other services and the national interest. Of that I had much experience. I can also remind you of the grossly arrogant and very dangerous US New Maritime Strategy which was a naval bid for dominance of the entire US defence field of a kind so far scarcely conceivable in this country. Dominance of the kind that is possible in Britain sustains jobs, profits for the defence industries and posts for the military, serving and retired. This, I suppose, is why the corrupt, secretive, authoritarian nuclear war culture chimes so elegantly with Thatcher's Britain. Conversely, the military mind never forgets the havoc to the status quo that a non-nuclear defence policy could do. That must impel them towards what Lord Zuckerman, once Chief Scientist to the Ministry of Defence and now a notable anti-nuclear dissident, called 'the ruthless, reckless momentum which can give an uncontrollable impetus over the next precipice in the board-room'. It keeps them aboard what the former Secretary of State for Defence Sir John Nott, ruefully describing his Ministry, saw as 'a huge supertanker, well captained, well engineered, well crewed, with the systems continually updated, but with no one ever asking where the hell it is going'.

From which, perhaps, it follows that expecting the military to do their duty in a way so radically different from what they currently conceive it to be is a tall order. And yet, and yet. What are the plusses in these daunting circumstances? First, there is nothing in what I briefly described of the transformation in Soviet strategy, the NATO non-response and the esconcing of the Bomb, so controversial that the military couldn't understand and react to it; it is there for all to perceive. Secondly, although I have strayed from the strictly military into the Tom Tiddler's ground of politics, that is what those who aim to be strategists above the colonels' level must do. Thirdly, although there are formidable problems, there is nothing insurmountably difficult about the way towards vanquishing the Bomb: common security, which is the dependence of each protagonist not on protection from the other but on a collaborative arrangement. It has been well explored in the military journals and internationally by an eminent commission headed by the late Olof Palme[76] as well as by well-founded bodies advocating it in various forms here and elsewhere, notably in West Germany, as one might expect. Its technicalities are no less comprehensible: the new military technologies do permit of weapons with ultra-precise capabilities and limitations which make them earnests of no-provocation-but-Heaven-help-you-if-you-do-any-provoking defence. They lend themselves to great steps forward in the difficult process of verification. They make obsolete the absurd idea of balance allowing, in a way that it cannot, for the differing situations and geography of the protagonists. It circumvents the trading of numbers and the separation of nuclear from non-nuclear negotiation by starting afresh from an assessment of the minimum force that the common security requirements of each protagonist, given weapon- and nuclear-free zones, could accept as sufficient. Fourthly, as the row in NATO about modernisation and compensation – that two or threefold multiple of new nuclear weapons that flows from INF – gets worse the flaws of the British posture as an American acolyte and a fraudulent claimant to nuclear independence will become more exposed; and with that will also appear the conviction that national *amour propre* can only be requited through the Bomb, and something will have to be found to take its place. That's a job for all those spare generals, with an emollient for hurt British post-empire, post-nuclear pride thrown in: British military genius emancipated at last, leading NATO towards common security and the two alliances out of the Bomb culture, the defeat.

That is an attitude change of an order familiar to medical professionals, who are just the people to help it along. The medical profession, if I may recall my time in health education, had to be bulldozed into accepting the inescapable logic of epidemiology and doing something about the smoking, alcohol abuse and doom-laden diet of the crass. The medical profession has the standing to bulldoze the military into accepting the inescapable logic of strategy and doing something about their doom-laden fixation on the Bomb – victory over a weapons system devoid of the human character of those footsore, careworn soldiers and entirely inhuman, rough-hewing not a century but eternity. Then, oh then, we would know what effect these men would have upon the enemy and, by God, they wouldn't frighten anyone. What an anxiolytic breakthrough that would be.

DISCUSSION
Question: What would be the effects on society and on the military if we returned to conscription for the armed forces?
Air Commodore Mackie: When we did have conscription it generally had a good effect on the military, broadening them, 'civilising' them and diluting the elite ethos. This may be partly why it was unpopular with professional soldiers and was eventually scrapped. But nowadays compulsory military service would only have bad effects, in my opinion. Techniques of training and manipulation have been refined so much it would only militarise society even more.

10

Soviet Perspectives

VALENTIN FOMICHEV

The insights into the military character, in particular its resistance to change, offered by the other contributors are of course true of the military everywhere. Political and ideological labels tend to mask these similarities. The quite astonishing similarities in attitude and outlook, in reaction to stress, to disagreement, and in resistance to change, are seldom commented upon in public discussion, nor are their implications reflected upon.

These military similarities of character present similar dangers to the societies in which they occur, and the degree of danger is determined by the degree to which the military drives the political. When military thinking determines or limits or unduly influences political thinking, as happens often, the whole country is shaped by the deficiencies of the military character. And the country's international relations also reflect the characteristic military deficiencies described elsewhere.

But we must not make the mistake of blaming the military servants for their political masters' failure to assert and insist upon values and policies which do serve their country's real, long-term interests. Perhaps it has been a general failure of political vision, by leaders of very many countries regardless of formal differences in ideology and allegiance, to realise how much countries' interests are interdependent in the long term. We prosper together, or we perish together, it is said. The catastrophic effects of nuclear weapons have served to highlight the basic fact that now, in the short term too, there cannot be winners and losers; either we all win together or we all lose together.

Until recently military thinking in the Soviet Union has suffered from the same lack of political vision and direction as in many other countries. Our own media suggested recently that the installation of SS20 missiles in the European part of USSR was at the insistence of our military, responding – as they saw it – to growing Western nuclear forces. This, if it is true, demonstrates how the military mirror each other and bring out the worst in each other, when they have too much influence, and increase the dangers we all live under. I will not pretend that all has changed completely in the Soviet Union, but there is certainly a process of change going on in Soviet political thinking which is being followed in military doctrine too.

Since 1945 both East and West have, in the name of defence, acquired nuclear and conventional arsenals which provide a massive offensive capability. In some cases defence strategies have included major offensive components and even, some would say, become indistinguishable from offensive strategies. For decades the recognition of another country's offensive capacity has prompted the increase in one's own offensive capacity. But we know now where this road is leading to.

In the Soviet Union today there is a fundamental change underway, with the armed forces moving towards an exclusively defensive role. The correctness of this change is not in dispute, although the methods by which it may be reached are still actively discussed and, sometimes, disagreed over.

I can explain this change in political and military thinking in terms of a switch from war-preparation to war-prevention. This new political thinking started in the mid-1980s, when it was realised that in the modern nuclear world, war, either with conventional or nuclear weapons, can never again be a possible option between major powers, if the planet is to survive. It follows from this that the offensive potential of a country's armed forces is of no practical use – it can only increase the danger of war by raising the level of uncertainty and sense of threat, and by making accident or miscalculation more likely. So the only way armed forces can actually prevent war is to have a wholly and exclusively defensive orientation. That is the nature of the change taking place in the Soviet military at the moment. Of course, it is a radical and difficult change to make. Institutions have an inertia, professions develop a characteristic way of perceiving the world and, at bottom, the soldier's calling of defending his homeland remains an honourable one – but not, it is now being recognised, by means which also destroy that home. Suicide is no defence.

There are also internal, domestic reasons for this change in military orientation, which make it more certain that the changes will be accomplished. The main aim of Soviet policy in general now is a thorough reconstruction of our society, removing the constraints which have caused great difficulties and dissatisfactions for us. This process can only go on in conditions of peace and security; the motivation or rationale for any external aggression simply does not exist in the USSR today.

This new defence-only thinking has the formal status of policy – no-one can pursue any other aims or policies. The focus of this policy is exclusively on war-prevention and what might be called 'defensive defence' to ensure the security of our country. The Soviet Union and Warsaw Pact have declared that they will not under any circumstances initiate any aggressive military action against other states. Any first-use or pre-emptive use of nuclear weapons is absolutely precluded.

This change is less a matter of changing political goals than of bringing military postures, and the attendant military technology, back into line with these political goals. After all, it is the Soviet Union which has been invaded from the West, not vice-versa, both during our Revolution and in the Second World War. With such vast loss of life and economic devastation, it is hardly surprising that fear of further invasion or aggression dominated Soviet military thinking in the years after 1945. In those early years we also heard many powerful voices in the USA calling for the use of atomic weapons against our still-devastated country, and acquiring similar weapons as quickly as possible seemed then the only chance of national survival.

Nowadays we operate on the basis that, for military forces to be truly defensive (that is, no threat to anyone), all countries should have a 'defence sufficiency' at the minimum level, and no more. Certainly not the existing gross excesses of armaments far beyond any conceivable defensive use. This means totally abandoning the new, dangerous concepts of nuclear war-fighting.

The difficulty is that, to achieve the true security of knowing that your neighbour does not have the means of attacking you, we need reciprocity in disarmament measures between countries. The Soviet Union has made, and is still making, unilateral cuts in its armed forces, but this reaches the point where a corresponding response is required. On the basis of reciprocity, the Soviet Union put forward and agreed the Intermediate Nuclear Forces Treaty ridding Europe of SS20s, SS23s, GLCMs, and Pershing missiles. The current Strategic Arms Reduction Talks are aimed at 50 per cent cuts in offensive strategic nuclear weapons. In April this year the Warsaw Pact suggested talks on reducing and eventually eliminating all tactical nuclear weapons in Europe, including nuclear components of dual-capable systems; in some of these, the Soviet Union has a numerical advantage currently. But it takes political will on both sides to make substantial progress towards a safer world; we can make the opening moves, but we cannot do this alone. Perhaps this recognition is growing in the West?

We believe that the phased reduction and eventual elimination of tactical nuclear weapons in Europe will not only reduce the risk of war, it will also strengthen trust and create a more stable situation. This will complement progress which we believe can be made towards the implementation of deep cuts in strategic nuclear and conventional forces and lead, in the long term, to the complete elimination of nuclear weapons. Instead of a delicately poised and ever-shifting military confrontation, our countries can live in peaceful coexistence, with greatly increased international cooperation – including in the military sphere. It is a dangerous view that denies the interests we have in common – including our basic survival – and forces our societies into a straitjacket defined by our differences.

I believe that the Medical Campaign Against Nuclear Weapons reflects the conviction of people everywhere, regardless of ideology and other differences, that we cannot collectively go any further down the nuclear road without unacceptable risks and unacceptable consequences.

11

A Diplomatic Conversion: from MAD to Mutual Assured Security

EDY J. KORTHALS ALTES

I resigned in 1986 as an Ambassador in the Dutch diplomatic service in order to warn the public that our present military policies have reached a point of great danger. It is essential that we change from the threat of Mutual Assured Destruction and its successor, nuclear war-fighting, to a constructive and unifying policy of Mutual Assured Security.

During the last five or six years of my career in the Dutch Foreign Service I became increasingly concerned at the ways in which the nuclear arms race was accelerating. I became convinced that we are fast approaching the point where the nature of our weapons and our new war-fighting policies make a nuclear holocaust virtually inevitable, the only uncertainty being when and exactly how it will start. For me the final straw was President Reagan's SDI, his grandiose 'Star-Wars' initiative. By this means the USA is attempting to become invulnerable to any Soviet retaliation whilst at the same time acquiring a nuclear first-strike capability in the context of nuclear war-fighting policies.

So I put my concerns on paper, as clearly as I could. This is not a healthy thing to do, career-wise, if you disagree with the political orthodoxy around nuclear weapons. The convention is that when senior diplomats disagree fundamentally with ministers, they must resign. I also wanted to free my hands to inform the public of what is going on and to work more fully and effectively for the changes which may, still, prevent this disaster. That is what I have been doing for the past three years.

This vital process of change involves moving from policies of Mutual Assured Destruction (MAD) and nuclear war-fighting to what I call Mutual Assured Security, in which the security of each side depends on the security of the other. Cooperation on economic, cultural and political levels should replace the current military confrontation.

There are four good reasons why we urgently need to change from MAD to Mutual Assured Security.

119

First, MAD does not, in fact, guarantee our security, (despite claims that it does and, absurdly, that it is the *only* way of being safe). On the contrary, it increases the risk we all live under, for several reasons. MAD and the nuclear mentality have produced two highly complex military systems which are opposed and antagonistic. It has been shown clearly that these military structures are unreliable, yet on their safe, error-free functioning depends the future of this planet, literally forever. They are unstable also because both Superpowers are engaged in a technology race, each trying to leapfrog the other with ever more destructive weapons. This is inherently destabilising. The Americans take the lead in this. Their new Stealth technology, for example, will allow nuclear bombers to evade radar detection. The resulting uncertainty and temptation to fear the worst in times of international tension have grave consequences for our security. It has been little appreciated in public that the great expenditures on research and development of new weapons systems are leading us further away from security into ever more dangerous waters.

The basic fact of our nuclear age is the vulnerability of everybody, everywhere, even in the most powerful nation in the world. No amount of arms spending is going to eliminate this basic reality. On the contrary, there is ample evidence that insecurity increases with the introduction of new and destabilising weapons-systems.

We live in a paradoxical, absurd situation: an enormous and steadily increasing input of scarce resources and human talent for ever more refined weapons which lead us to greater insecurity! Both Soviet and American scientists[46] have come to the same conclusion, saying: 'We can no longer allow the survival of civilisation to be dependent on the error-free operation of high technology defence systems – or on the rational functioning of sometimes irrational human beings.'

Unfortunately, our military and political leaders are not listening to these warnings. We must make them listen.

Secondly, MAD leads to the proliferation of weapons of indiscriminate mass destruction, whether nuclear or chemical. The perfecting and miniaturisation of nuclear weapons prevent us restricting their deployment to a small, exclusive club of First World nations. More and more countries are following the abysmal example set by the Superpowers and their allies. We can't blame them: if we claim we are safe only by possessing nuclear weapons, then logically every country in the world should have them! Chemical weapons are also becoming more widespread. They are comparatively cheap and easy to produce; if a country cannot afford nuclear technology but wants the power and prestige and security with which we justify them, chemical weapons are the next best alternative. But these developments, for which the Superpowers are largely responsible, greatly increase the devastation caused in regional conflicts. They also increase the risk of regional wars spreading more widely and escalating in seriousness. This appalling prospect should stimulate our thinking about the urgent need to establish a new and constructive relationship between East and West to halt this process and minimise its existing consequences.

An effective United Nations is essential for the responsible management of the complex threats to the survival of our small planet. New East–West relations based on Mutual Assured Security and cooperation instead of confrontation are essential preconditions for an effective United Nations. The need has never been greater.

Thirdly, a durable and constructive approach dealing with East–West problems cannot be based on MAD. Military thinking has dominated East–West relations for decades, but the political problems we face cannot be solved by military means. The military-security aspects can no longer be considered on their own merits; instead they must be integrated within the framework of a broad peace policy. What is happening now is exactly the opposite. Our governments are talking in Brussels about a 'comprehensive concept' covering what new nuclear weapons we need in the coming years. Public opinion is misled by this misuse of the term – it is not comprehensive because it is limited to military matters. Everything else is subsumed to the military character of the East–West confrontation, and account is not taken of the full extent of East–West relations. Instead, we should approach East–West relations from an inclusive and integrating point of view.

Fourthly, our growing 'MADness' not only diminishes our chances of dealing effectively with two major threats to our security but actually increases the dangers we face. The appalling Third World problems and the rapid destruction of our natural environment require immediate common action from East and West. But instead we spend US $100 billion on the arms race every year, to no good purpose.

While we are playing with these highly expensive toys in one room, the house is being set on fire from two sides, by environmental degradation and by mounting Third World crises. In environmental terms we are being appallingly bad parents, handing on to our children a planetary life-system which is breaking down under the burdens we continue to inflict on it. And each day we choose to spend the economic fruits of that environmental plunder on armaments instead of alleviating the terrible suffering of our brothers and sisters in the Third World.

Very recently a little more concern has been shown for the environmental results of our behaviour, but in comfortably limited ways which don't touch on the role of vast military spending. There is even a tendency, which politicians find convenient, for people to turn their attention from matters of war and peace to the environment. But the two are inextricably linked. As well as wasting vast sums of money, Cold War thinking itself results in major pollution of the planet.

When politicians in the West talk of a 'happy mix of conventional and nuclear weapons', they must know this is not true. We are sacrificing true environmental security for an illusory military security.

Towards Mutual Assured Security

Security can no longer be guaranteed on a purely national basis nowadays, as the Palme Commission[76] has shown us. It can only be realised in cooperation with the potential opponent.

This could be achieved if the Superpowers would accept that the security of each depends on the security of the other. For us Europeans, whether East or West, it is very important that we see that there is no security other than Mutual Assured Security in our small, densely populated and highly vulnerable continent.

Mutual Assured Security means: 'I am secure if you are secure', and vice-versa. This only exists if my position in its totality (weapons, structure, strategy, deployment, logistics, etc.) is not perceived as threatening the other side by giving me an offensive capability.

In mutual security there is, therefore, a clear element of reciprocity. It is in each other's interests to reduce those military elements that may be interpreted as menacing. This implies first accepting the other state whether we like its regime or not; and secondly, refraining from actions to impose our will or from seeking superiority via a decisive breakthrough in arms-technology.

The replacement of the outdated concept of national security by the concept of Mutual Assured Security represents a Copernican change in relations between the two European power-blocs. The time has come for an agonising and urgent reappraisal of the present course to disaster. A restating of the basic concept of security is therefore of crucial importance. The reality of today demands a total rejection of the basic concept of nuclear and conventional deterrence. The ultimate consequence of continuation along these lines is not security but the actual achievement of mutual assured destruction.

The concept of Mutual Assured Security can be translated into concrete actions directed towards the following:

First, a halt to the quantitative and qualitative arms-race. If we accept that war between the two blocs is no longer winnable, and that threat of war can no longer be considered as a tool of policy, there is no longer any need to continue the arms-race. Modernising and further development of nuclear arms no longer makes any sense. But there are still powerful forces in Western Europe and the USA which will not accept this. It needs to become generally accepted that no form of war is a reasonable option between East and West. The chances of any conflict remaining limited in area or weapons used are very slight. Any conflict in Europe would surely result in the total obliteration of both sides, with dire consequences for the rest of the world. If we grasp these points, which are inescapable, the only solution is a radical break with the old, pre-nuclear ways of thinking which have got us into this situation.

Second, drastic reductions of existing nuclear weapons to a minimum level, and elimination of chemical and biological weapons are also essential, as is our third goal, reduction and restructuring of all conventional forces in order to make a surprise attack highly improbable.

Nato and the Warsaw Pact

The concept of Mutual Assured Security should be implemented in the context of the two alliances, NATO and the Warsaw Pact. I think we need to continue with these two organisations, in order to transform them. A restructuring of NATO and building of a much more independent European component are essential, in order to persuade US politicians and military planners to adopt far more constructive approaches. The time has come for a bold initiative from European countries which could be of decisive importance for this radical change in East–West relations. Such an independent initiative is becoming more possible, as more people realise that the greatest concentration of the means of mass destruction is located in our small and densely populated continent. The security interests of the Superpowers are not always identical with the vital interests of all European states in mutual survival. These are good reasons to strive for a much greater European influence on the vital issues affecting our security. European security depends on the relations between the two Superpowers. If these worsen, we suffer; if they improve we will benefit. There is no nuclear sanctuary called Europe today!

From Confrontation Towards Cooperation

Science and technology, as well as the great vulnerability of our modern societies, leave us no other choice than to replace the old concept 'If you want peace, prepare for war.'

The reality of today demands therefore the adoption of a completely different maxim: 'If you don't want war, prepare for peace.' This means the development of a broad peace policy on the basis of a truly comprehensive concept that integrates all aspects of the very complex relations between East and West, instead of allowing military aspects to predominate, as now. In fact the West's 'modernisation' of nuclear weapons now in process is yet another attempt to mislead the public – it is not mere modernisation, it is a dangerous escalation of the arms race. This is a grotesque abuse of language, and of the democratic process: what are being introduced are new, more 'efficient' and destabilising nuclear weapons.

The military aspects should therefore be integrated within a total concept which comprises five major components: military, political, economic, cultural and humanitarian, as well as cooperation on environmental issues and the Third World. This comprehensive approach prioritising cooperation instead of confrontation calls for simultaneous action in all fields; and progress in one field may have positive consequences in another area. This interaction between the various elements could have a decisive influence on the elimination of distrust and suspicion that still linger in all military negotiations. The integrated approach permits a radical change in international relations and thus contributes to a reduction of the military threat and greater real security on both sides.

One important aspect is economic cooperation, not just in credit and capital but also between monetary and trading institutions East and West such as the IMF, GATT, and the OECD, with joint ventures and much increased trade. At present trade is minimal – the Netherlands for example exports a mere 1.5 per cent to the Soviet Union. A much fuller intertwining of economic interests will be a part of Mutual Assured Security, as well as much more extensive cultural contacts.

A Reorientation of Human Consciousness

There is one thing which we would do well to remember. All our reasonable, intelligent concepts such as the comprehensive test ban, Mutual Assured Security and the integrated approach will come to nothing if they are not supported by a profound change of mind. The West German physicist and philosopher Carl Friedrich von Weizsäcker is right when he puts so much emphasis on the urgent need for 'Bewustseinswandel', a deep change in our consciousness. So we need a fundamental reorientation of human consciousness. This involves starting to think more for ourselves on these basic issues. We need to reclaim an individual responsibility and exercise the right and duty to say that the existing military and political order is irresponsible and, having demonstrably failed, must change.

In each of the three global problems (peace, the environment, and the Third World) an immediate and drastic change of our course of action is essential if we want to avoid a catastrophe. The dramatic worsening of the situation in the Third World is a reality. The death and hunger, the extreme poverty of millions of our brothers and sisters should be an unacceptable scandal for us living in the prosperous North. Of great concern also is the rapidly worsening destruction of our natural environment. We should, by now, know that if we are not prepared to take adequate measures we are destroying the prospects of life for our children. But unless we stop our senseless, criminal arms race there will be no hope of coping in an efficient way with these grave problems. Rational concepts, however, are not enough. Nothing less than a fundamental reorientation of our thinking, especially in the 'highly developed North', will be required. There is an urgent need for cooperation among the great religions – together with the humanistic tradition – in order to provide us with the essential elements for this reorientation.

In this process of rethinking and the critical review of our acting and lifestyles, we would be well advised to listen carefully to the essence of the Message that for so many centuries was proclaimed in East and West. Jesus Christ not only preached about a different and fuller life. He actually lived a life of love. He makes a new life, a new beginning, a radical reorientation possible. Modern technology forces us to listen, much more carefully than before, to His Sermon of the Mount. Jesus Christ was never exclusive, always inclusive.

We must become fully conscious in a moral and spiritual sense, so that this permeates the political sphere – there is no other way to escape from the annihilation threatening us. We must awake to our basic individual responsibility of removing these failures of our political organisation, and stop condoning – if only from our silence and inaction – their dangerous and unjust consequences in the world today. We must, and can, cooperate around Albert Schweitzer's tenet of respect for all life. This means we must say 'no' to MAD and 'yes' to Mutual Assured Security.

DISCUSSION

Question: We seem to be saying that now the point has suddenly been reached where it is wrong to spend such vast amounts on weapons of mass destruction, instead of alleviating Third World poverty and saving the environment. But this has always been true – for the last 30 years I have watched fortunes spent on the nuclear arsenals which are at last terrifying us into a semblance of sanity while for decades millions of people in the Third World have starved or died of preventable diseases. Should we not recognise that we have already done great wrong, particularly those people with more power than we will ever have, some of whom are suddenly realising the dangers facing themselves too?

Drs Korthals Altes: I agree, and I think that makes even stronger the arguments for stopping this criminal madness now. But it works both ways – it is also difficult for people to admit that for decades they have been part of a cruel and oppressive system. We have to make it easier for them to admit this. Society hides this truth from all of us, so we don't begin to realise what has been going on until our adult lives are formed, with all the usual material commitments that make it very hard for people to change. We are misled into investing in the system, but it is hard to disinvest.

Question: So much of the arms race bypasses the normal democratic processes in that new weapons arrive before we have a chance to express our disgreement. Air-launched Cruise will soon be deployed at USAF Upper Heyford near Oxford, circumventing the INF Treaty. But amongst these so-called modernisations is the Follow-on To Lance. This is one dangerous development we can possibly influence because it is some way from deployment and the final decisions have yet to be made.

Drs Korthals Altes: As well as protesting against these dangerous developments, which I agree have not been sanctioned democratically, we must offer positive, substantial alternatives, and insist our governments come up with a constructive, comprehensive peace policy which is *not* based on an arms race and arms sales to the Third World. We must show the benefits for everyone of moving from confrontation to cooperation, and how such a move can be made.

Question: Surely the way forward is for us all to unite in much greater numbers, to demand real democracy in Britain. It is the lack of true democracy which has produced the situation we all complain of and which keeps the widespread opposition to nuclear arms on the sidelines of society.

Dr Hanna Segal: That process of gaining more democratic accountability has started – at least, the need for it is recognised much more widely now. But as we press for this, and for nuclear disarmament, we must be realistic if we wish to succeed. We must realise the vested interests we are up against, the military-industrial complex, for example. This makes vast profits from arms sales to the Third World. New weapons are made more affordable to Western governments by selling large quantities to the Third World, which is where they are actually used. The role of the USA and other major countries in this, which we often overlook in our focus on nuclear weapons, must be made known to the general public and opposed.

Drs Korthals Altes: It is obscene that profits are made out of death, and on such a huge, systematic basis. I wonder if nationalisation of the arms industry is not the only way of controlling this. We also need to work out how people employed in the arms industries could be re-employed elsewhere. Economists have shown that arms manufacture creates less employment than many other industries and services, so this should be possible. But this needs to be understood more widely.

12

Exchange and Change

ARMORER WASON

Much of my work consists of bringing people from the UK and USSR together. Effective exchange between our two countries – ideally the building of continued, dynamic, mutually valuable relationships – has much to offer us. It is not a substitute for political change, but it does help to bring this about. We are only at the beginning of really tapping this, but we are learning how to set up structures to maximise contact.

There has been a great increase in activity between our two countries and in the quality of exchange. There have been particularly exciting developments in youth exchange, perhaps from the unexpected quarters. During his visit to the Soviet Union last year the UK's Minister of Education, Kenneth Baker, and the Soviet Minister for Education set up a rolling programme of school exchanges whereby 2,000 young people will visit their counterparts in the next two years and stay in each others' homes. The Society for Cultural Relations with the USSR which brings young people from Britain and the USSR together each year is focussing in 1989 on involving the young people in ecological and environmental projects. Twinning visits (such as that described in the SPINA evaluation in Appendix I) are including more determined attempts at equal opportunity recruitment, thorough preparation of the young people for the trip and follow-up afterwards. We are learning about the kinds of structure that promote high quality exchange and provide for the widest possible participation. In Britain we are yet to treat it, however, as the important, high profile activity that it has become in many parts of the USA. Given that this is so, I want to focus on the significance of East–West exchange as a way forward at the personal level.

It may be instructive to see how I, personally, became involved in this work. I come from an upper-middle-class background. My parents had not lost their ideals but were still children of their class. I learnt Russian at school from the age of twelve, was captivated by my loving, unjudgemental and expressive Russian teacher, and threw myself into the culture. I eventually went to work in the Soviet Union and strangely felt more at home, and more accepted, than I had in England. I came back to England in 1981. In an attempt to reclaim my roots in this country, and to try and understand my confusion, I spent five years here and in the USA as a social worker and counsellor. I only realised a few years ago that, as a combination of skills, this was extremely useful.

The question we are all asking is: 'Peace is abroad, yet the arms race continues. Why?'. We have been striving to understand what prompts people in key decision-making roles to continue to support nuclear arms and why people vote for governments that do so. Some of the psychological mechanisms we encounter when we seek to make it possible for people to change their minds have been described in earlier chapters. Clearly, offering information is not enough in itself. It seems to me that two things are needed. We need to create opportunities for people to see the reality of the situation, to combat our narrowness and realise that our enemy images are a sham. And we need the close support of people who will not be hostile towards us as we do this, because it is in itself a traumatic process.

Effective exchange between people from Britain and the USSR has enormous potential to achieve these aims. We live our lives with little idea of how divided we are from other cultures, and indeed within our own country. Soviet people are much more aware of the East–West divide, long for contact with us and, given the opportunity, bring home very forcefully to us the degree of separation that we have grown used to. The enormous interest in and warmth towards us that Russians often express counters our cultural isolation and narrowness and often brings about a re-examination of attitudes. The experience can be cathartic, and can lead to action. I have experienced many examples of this.

I often take groups of specialist workers to meet their counterparts in the USSR. I recently took a group of pre-school workers to a very rapturous welcome in a nursery unused to foreigners. I went to the cloakroom at one point to find five or six young British women weeping and holding on to each other. 'We had no idea', they said. They returned to the nursery that evening and organised the beginnings of an exchange between nurseries. One of the things we need to do is push through our timidity and particularly our embarrassment about making contact. I took a group of social workers to the Soviet Union last year. One of them sat on a crowded trolleybus and involved the Russians around her in her attempts to pronounce the cyrillic alphabet. This led to contact with a man pioneering outreach work with young people in Leningrad, with whom ten of the British social workers have set up an information exchange. They are now planning their next steps in East–West work.

It may be that those of us whose work revolves around people find it easier to make the kind of contact I am talking about. But it can be a profound and unexpected experience for all kinds of people. Last year I interpreted for a group of musicians from Siberia on a short tour of Britain. This was very illuminating for me. I have got used to the warmth and interest that Soviet people meet in Hackney and in the North of England, particularly Sheffield, which has one of the most successful and lively twinning relationships with a Soviet city. However it was with some trepidation that I set off southwards with this group to stay amongst families in a small town in Surrey, not far from Farnham, Aldershot and Sandhurst. I had become extremely fond of this group who were particularly friendly, natural and close-knit. Music is an excellent way to bypass barriers and this group revelled in impromptu performances. At the motorway service station they played and danced in the car park to welcoming hoots from passing lorry drivers and the amazement of a coachload of elderly people.

We arrived and were distributed among families whom it seemed had been selected on the basis of how clean their homes were. The Soviets did not like being separated but were intrigued rather than upset by the lack of welcome. I also stayed in a family and found myself wrestling with what seemed to me their superficial interests, fixed opinions, and dedication to succeed in a business that seemed to me not to create anything of value. I was dismayed, but I noticed that I was finding it much more difficult than were the Soviets. They began to make friends, found places to sit and play, including in the local pub, and threw themselves into a concert that had been arranged for them. The town began to take an increasing interest in them and their English hosts began to wonder what they could do in return. At a reception organised for them the British administrator broke down and cried on and off for the rest of the evening. On their farewell morning host-families, well-wishers and Soviet visitors sang 'We Shall Overcome' outside the village pub, tears rolling down their faces. The Soviet group had reached the people of this small town far more effectively and quickly than any form of political activity I can think of.

Talking to them had also helped me understand the motivations and fears of the people we were staying with and enabled me to see them far more sympathetically. The experience brought home to me how little we have penetrated our own divisions. Exchange between Britain and the USSR also produces practical opportunities for us to provide support for a people and a country at present involved in a massive and brave attempt at change. Much is already happening, and of course more needs to happen, in the exchange of ideas, ways of working and technologies. To single out one obvious example, the UK–USSR Medical Exchange is doing extremely valuable work. But I want to concentrate on how we can be helpful at a personal level.

For people in the West, frustrated with the difficulty of bringing about political change, Mikhail Gorbachev is a source of hope and inspiration. We are so keen to cling on to this that it makes it hard for us to get an accurate picture of what is happening now in the Soviet Union and to listen to what Soviet people are telling us.

The present period in the USSR is an extraordinarily painful and difficult one. A friend said 'It feels like the anaesthetic wearing off after the operation.' Feelings of despair are just below the surface for nearly everyone. The artistic community may be flowering, but it is also seeing a sharp increase in suicides. My understanding of this is that these feelings are not born of what is happening at present but are surging up from long years of being 'anaesthetised'. Perhaps it is because there is now some hope and possibilities for change that people are experiencing this. However, many are assuming that the despair is real, that perestroika is doomed. There are very serious difficulties with it, but cynicism and despair are not a good position from which to bring perestroika about. I think we have a very valuable role to play in listening to what is happening and in gently offering our encouragement and thoughts on what we see as the reality.

Similarly, for many it is very hard to feel any sense of pride. Confronting their past has brought a welter of shame and worthlessness. It is valuable for us to point out how brave we think they are being, that we also have not come to terms with aspects of our past and are far from realising our democratic ideals. Just as we have romantic notions about what is happening in the Soviet Union, we need to correct their romantic notions about the West. We need to encourage them to assume that they will develop their own solutions, rather than look to us for ours. We must be careful about importing into the USSR our ideas and technologies. With our colonial past, and despite our good intentions, we run the risk of acting from the unaware assumption that we know best.

There are difficulties to which we need to find creative joint solutions. One thing that adversely affects our relationships is the economic and material differences between our countries. Some Soviets are oblivious to these differences. The Siberian musicians gave away to buskers in the London Underground much of the tiny amount of hard currency they were allowed to exchange. For others it is hard to be with foreigners who seem to have everything, and this may affect how they relate to us.

There are plenty of other challenges, but it is the process of working together to solve them that cements our relationships East and West. Opportunities for contact and exchange have never been greater, and the value to all of us is far-reaching.

DISCUSSION

Question: I wondered how we could show the human reality behind the enemy image which has been fixed on the Soviet Union, so we tried to twin Horsham with a Soviet town. I work and live in West Sussex, which has the highest Conservative majority in the country. But we are making great progress in this twinning arrangement. There's a lot of support even in this area. Twinning our towns with towns in France, Germany etc., is common now, so do you think that twinning with USSR could be done by many towns and cities in this country?

Armorer Wason: I do, and I think we should have the highest expectations of Conservative supporters and avoid our own version of the enemy image. People generally live up or down to your expectations of them. In promoting this we can point to a very recent initiative of this government in setting up a programme of school exchanges. This is very ambitious: 50 school partnerships at this stage, with 80 per cent of them state schools, and a further 200 on the waiting list. These schools are making contact with their partner-schools in the USSR already, sending letters, tapes, photographs, exchanging teachers before the visit, and involving the community. It is worth everyone finding out which local schools are doing this and offering support, from a clearly non-political standpoint. Teachers are probably badly supported in this, and could do with help in preparation to make sure these exchanges are as productive as possible.

Afterword

IAN MUNRO

About 40 years ago I was confronted by an early breed of the nuclear mentality in its rawest mood. In the officers' mess of a British military hospital a colonel was condemning the latest intransigences of the Soviet Union. He had no doubt of what should be done: a surprise attack on the communists with what was then called the Bomb, which it was believed the Russians did not possess at that time. Forgetting my lowly rank, I protested angrily and described such a course of action as monstrous. I was put sharply in my place and perhaps my military record was inscribed with a symbol indicating a serious security risk.

I am reminded by some of the contributions to this book that the colonel's attitude may be far from obsolete, at any rate in the thoughts of some Western decision-makers, though it has, like much of the weaponry it brandishes, been modernised as the nuclear arms race has advanced. Now that missile-guidance systems can achieve pinpoint targeting and probably destroy all identified weapons silos; now that the US Navy believes it can dispose of Soviet submarines in 'the first five minutes' (as Air Commodore Mackie explained in Chapter 9); and now that the illusion of the Strategic Defence Initiative promises a shelter against whatever depleted counterattack might be mounted by a Soviet Union crippled after an unexpected nuclear bombardment, then the vision may be sustained in the Pentagon and in NATO of an enemy almost as comfortingly vulnerable and bereft of power to retaliate as it seemed to that colonel in 1948.

Here is the hardened bunker of a technologically updated nuclear mentality, perhaps softened slightly by the slow acceptance of the possibility that the Superpowers might come to terms over sharing the world in watchful tolerance, if not immediately in full harmony and cooperation. But any setback in the process of dismantling East–West confrontation could bring on a resurgence of the nuclear arms race, urged forward by those for whom the latest refinements in weapons and their delivery mean that a nuclear war is fightable and winnable. So long as the world is burdened by the years of mistrust, based on old-fashioned ideas of incompatibility of ideologies, and by a legacy of deep-rooted hostility, so long will deterrence by vast nuclear arsenals hold its appeal, though it could be said that President Gorbachev has gone a long way towards rendering deterrence obsolete. However that may be, what, if anything, can a *medical* campaign do to accelerate the reversal of these ways of thinking and to dispel the acceptance they receive from so many citizens of the nuclear powers?

Anton Obholzer in Chapter 3 examined how personal and social defence mechanisms constantly supply a denial that encroaches on awareness of the nuclear threat. And denial becomes all the easier in the aftermath of moderately successful negotiations towards reduction of nuclear arms, though the agreed cut is a trivial 4 per cent in the case of the INF Treaty. This does virtually nothing to lift the danger of a nuclear exchange precipitated inadvertently as the result of human instability or error. So the campaign's message, unpopular though it may be to many of those to whom it is directed, must continue to include foremost the exposure of denial that the threat still exists. Dr Obholzer believes that the best way of strengthening resolve in this renewed effort is mutual support in small groups and organisations. To that must be added the awareness that such assemblies will be no more than congregations of the converted unless they can carry their arguments effectively into wider public and political arenas.

Alastair Mackie (Chapter 9) maintains that those who present the medical case against the accumulation of nuclear arms have the standing to induce change in the military mind and to dispel its fixation on nuclear weapons. I am less hopeful: Air Commodore Mackie's own portrayal of the closed and disciplined hierarchy of the armed forces illustrates how hard it will be to shift the military advisers and decision-makers from their convictions. But so long as they have their political masters they can be influenced from above; and it is to those above that the pressure must be directed, through whatever democratic process may be available and whichever unhampered journalists and broadcasters may be on hand to relay the warning.

One of the chapters which is particularly interesting is Scilla Elworthy's report (Chapter 7) of the Oxford Research Group's enquiries amongst British nuclear decision-makers – military, political, scientific, and bureaucratic. Among them, it was deduced, certain assumptions prevailed: notably, that regardless of the threat from the Soviet Union the Western powers must maintain and modernise their nuclear arsenals; that accidental war and escalation can never happen; and that all decision-makers are always rational and always in control of the weapons. Powerful medical arguments question some of these assumptions – especially the total freedom from risk of accident and the assumed guarantee of rational behaviour in all conceivable circumstances. The political mentality which lays long-rooted confidence in deterrence and ever more deterrence by ever more destructive warheads must be assailed by these and all the other medical arguments, applied in today's more hopeful atmosphere.

Eventually, recognition may dawn that a new element has entered the balance: deterrence and huge nuclear arsenals will truly become irrelevant when each Superpower convinces the other that it speaks of disarmament in earnest and in good faith, and that it no longer stands as a glowering threat from which there is no release. That is the fundamental precept in all attempts to denuclearise mentalities. At the moment, acceptance of the startling notion that true security does *not* derive from nuclear weapons requires a preliminary act of faith and trust; and the expression of any such novel sentiments towards an antagonist long identified as a menace will draw condemnation from those who cannot contemplate any change from the 'comfort' of Mutual Assured Destruction. The ultimate achievement of the goal of mutual security, of which Drs Korthals Altes speaks in Chapter 11, will demand supranational cooperation on a scale and depth hitherto dismissed as unattainable. The process towards such security cannot be presented to governments and peoples as free from risk. But for the past four decades, since my encounter with that colonel, the outlook for the advancement of humanity in every land has been overshadowed by perils of hideous magnitude. So far, the worst has not befallen, though the morbid impact of the nuclear arms race has been apparent. But the worst might still happen – if rigidity and suspicion freeze the mind and we continue to seek security in the means of our destruction.

Appendix I

An Evaluation of a Visit to the Soviet Union by Young People from Hackney, London

HEATHER HUNT, MICHAEL ORGEL, LESLEY MORRISON and
ARMORER WASON (SPINA)

Introduction

Hackney Council is one of 14 local authorities in the United Kingdom that is twinned with a district in the USSR. Hackney is twinned with Krasnaya Presnya, an industrial district of Moscow. One aim of the twinning arrangement is to develop understanding between the peoples of the two communities. A key part of the twinning programme has been exchange visits of young people. Hackney youngsters first took part in an exchange visit in the summer of 1986. Fifteen young Muscovites were hosted by Hackney in the summer of 1987 and in August 1988 13 young Hackney people and two adult leaders were invited to the Soviet Union as guests of Krasnaya Presnya.

The Study Group on Psychosocial Issues in the Nuclear Age (SPINA) became interested in evaluating exchange visits to assess how this kind of direct experience with Soviet young people affects attitudes towards the Soviet Union, helps develop a broader international perspective, and affects the young people's hopes and fears for the future.

One of the SPINA members (H.H.) has been involved in developing Hackney's twinning arrangements and through this connection Hackney Council gave permission for a SPINA research team to evaluate the visit. The twinning officer and SPINA members have worked closely together implementing an equal opportunities policy in advertising and selection for the trip. Thirteen youngsters were selected aged 12 to 15, six girls and seven boys. They attended different schools and the group reflected the cultural and ethnic diversity of Hackney. Eight were from black or ethnic minority communities. They were accompanied by two adult leaders, one a member of SPINA who is fluent in Russian and knows the Soviet Union well, the other an experienced secondary school teacher. The leaders and twinning officer held six preparatory meetings for the young people and their parents before they

139

went so the young people could get to know each other and their leaders, learn what would be expected of them, some basic information about Soviet society and a few words of Russian, and support each other in fundraising.

The young people were in the Soviet Union for three weeks as guests of the Executive Committee of Krasnaya Presnya. They stayed at a Young Pioneer Camp about 25 miles outside Moscow for 20 days. Young people from Moscow and other parts of the USSR were at the camp. The Hackney group ate together in the dining room and were allocated space in a dormitory, but there was plenty of opportunity for joint sporting, cultural and other informal activities. The leaders were able to help facilitate as much communication as possible, and many of the Soviet youngsters spoke English. A few days were spent on day trips to Krasnaya Presnya and other parts of Moscow for sightseeing, cultural visits and visits to museums offering opportunities to learn about Soviet history.

The Hackney youngsters spent the last two days of the visit as guests of families in the Krasnaya Presnya district of Moscow.

Pilot Study
In order to develop useful evaluation measures a pilot study was undertaken. The Head Teacher of an Inner London Girls' Comprehensive School agreed for a SPINA research team to interview pupils before and after a week's school trip to Leningrad and Moscow in February 1988. Eleven pupils in the age range 15 to 17 volunteered to be interviewed. Interviews were conducted approximately ten days before and ten days after the trip.[54]

Nature of the Sample
Participants in both this and the pilot study were not randomly drawn from their schools but were self-selected, composed of young people particularly interested in travel, and perhaps the Soviet Union. They were probably atypical in many ways. The aims of the study focus on the changes in attitudes and knowledge of these particular young people and the processes involved. Their initial attitudes cannot be taken as representative of young people of their age.

Aims and Method

- To describe the attitudes of the 13 to 15 year-old Hackney participants towards the Soviet Union, their image of life in the

Soviet Union, their attitude towards international relations, and their hopes and fears for the future, both before and after the visit.

- To describe any changes in their attitudes, images, hopes and fears after the visit.
- To gain knowledge of any of their experiences which influenced their attitudes, knowledge, hopes and fears during the visit.
- To give the participants an opportunity to think in advance about their trip in a constructive way and, on their return, reflect on their experiences.
- To use the information gained to contribute to the development of good practice guidelines for youth exchanges and visits to the USSR.

One (A.W.) of the group leaders' perspectives is included following the formal evaluation as a complementary source of descriptions and ideas based on her practical experience.

Twelve of the 13 young people were interviewed individually during the ten days before the visit and within ten days of their return. They were interviewed after their preparatory meetings to ensure that any changes found in the post-visit interviews would reflect only the impact of the visit itself. (One young person was on holiday immediately before his departure so was unavailable for interview.) There was no formal evaluation of changes in attitudes and knowledge as a consequence of the preparatory meetings. Semi-structured interviews were developed based on the pilot study. The interviewers were a child psychotherapist, a clinical psychologist, a research psychologist, a medical doctor and a community physician, all participating in the study on a voluntary basis. All were trained in the interview to ensure comparability. The leader (A.W.), who is also a SPINA member, did not participate in the interviewing in order to avoid any subtle influencing of attitudes. With one exception, a different person interviewed the young people on their return, and these interviewers were not acquainted with the young person's responses in their pre-trip interview. With the exception of two post-visit interviews conducted in the home of one of the interviewers, the interviews were conducted on council premises, took between 30 and 40 minutes and were recorded.

Interview Technique and Analysis

The interviews were semi-structured. Pre- and post-interviews had comparable questions to elicit information on four areas: (1) images and attitudes towards the USSR; (2) their own hopes and fears for the future; (3) knowledge of Soviet involvement in the Second World War; (4) attitudes towards international relations including nuclear policy. The pre-interview also included some 'priming' questions to help focus their interest and perception. Post-interviews had questions to elicit the nature of the young people's contacts with Soviet youngsters and what effect that had. Interviewers offered prompts to help elicit and focus responses. Non-leading questions were asked, such as 'Can you say a bit more about that?' and 'In what way?' to clarify meaning when there was an ambiguous response.

The analysis is essentially descriptive. There was no comparison control and numbers are too small for statistical analysis.

The interview had seven open-ended questions covering the four areas noted above. The responses gave opportunities to code them into categories; these categories were developed from the themes that had emerged from the more in-depth interviews conducted in the pilot study.

There were also two closed yes/no type questions. Responses were grouped to assess any change between the pre- and post-interview. Seven of the questions in the pre- and eleven in the post-interview were open-ended without predetermined categories. This allowed for description of the participants' own particular interests, experiences and ideas.

Decisions on coding interview responses were made by two of the research team jointly (M.O., H.H.) and checked independently by a third (L.M.). Any difference was discussed and the response coded into a category agreed by all three of the research teams.

Description of the Twelve Participating Young People Interviewed

There were six girls, and six boys. Their ages ranged from 12 to 15, eight were 15 years old, one 14, two 13 and one 12. Eleven were British, and one a citizen of Kenya. In accordance with the London Borough of Hackney's equal opportunities policy the participants were asked 'to which ethnic group would you say you belong'. Ten choices were offered including 'other/specify'. The responses are shown in Table Appendix I.

Table Appendix I. Ethnic Groupings (self-selected) of 12 Young
People Interviewed

UK black	4
African and UK black	1
White	3
Turkish	2
Asian	1
Other/Jewish (not orthodox)	1

These choices gave participants an opportunity to self-identify to
which ethnic group they belonged. The responses reflect the ethnic
diversity of the group. In the pre-trip interview the young people
were asked if they got a daily newspaper at home. Eleven of the
twelve replied they had daily papers at home. Seven had the *Daily
Mirror*, two the *Guardian*, one the *Independent* and one the *Daily
Mail*.

Results

Attitudes and Images of the Soviet Union
The number of interviewees who gave a particular response was
recorded. Several interviewees gave more than one category of
response so the total number of responses exceeds the number of
interviewees.

Responses to question: *What do you think Soviet society is like? Do
you have any images or ideas?*
Pre-visit: The most common ideas and images (four responses) were
about expectations of lifestyle and culture. A theme emerged of
anticipated quietness and of things being 'old-fashioned'. One said
she expected it to be 'clean and tidy'. Three interviewees were
reluctant to voice stereotypes: 'I think you only hear about bad bits
– it puts across the image that they just want power'; 'I've heard
that all women over there are body-builders – I don't know how
true that is. They wear those funny hats. They're all probably stereotypes'; 'I don't have any ideas. That's why I'm going. I don't
automatically accept what the press says.'
   Three interviewees offered images with a political accent which
varied from thinking that 'everyone marched round Red Square' to
there being 'a lot of politics going on in the country'. One answer
from a participant who had been to Eastern Europe previously

implied an image about repression – 'Me and my Mum passed through Moscow Airport – and saw guards with long coats and guns.'

Three voiced ideas about shortages and economic constraints: 'not having lots of things we have, washing machines, fashionable clothes'; 'less of everything we've got'; 'all the luxuries and things we take for granted they don't seem to have.'

Post-visit: Eight interviewees, as opposed to two pre-trip, described the qualities of the people. The word 'friendly' was used by six people. Other descriptions included 'warm-hearted', 'very loving', 'nice to be with', 'caring', 'stuff you with food and won't take no for an answer', and 'hospitable'.

An awareness of the extent of social fairness and more equal distribution of wealth seemed to have developed during the trip. No-one commented on this aspect pre-visit but four did so post-visit: 'People all seemed the same, more equal.' However, there was a sense of disappointment from some participants that they had not stayed with 'ordinary' families: 'When we were in the camp we saw how kids really lived. In two days in the family we found out how it wasn't. They set us up with rich families, with Persian carpets, TV, record players, and caviar.'

The number of people referring to shortages was unchanged (three respondents) although only one did so both before and after the trip. Only one person before and one after the trip commented on individual opportunities for Soviets: 'Teenage life might be restricted' (before) and 'strong academic emphasis without scope for creativity is a setback for people' (after).

Responses to question: *What do you think the good aspects are?*
Pre-visit: Social fairness was the aspect of Soviet society perceived as good most often before the trip (four young people): 'There are not very rich and very poor people'; 'They share the money they make and distribute it'; 'Equality of people – not materially but in terms of value placed on the individual'; 'more settled – maybe because they're communist.'

Three young people did not know what to expect. Three referred to aspects of society relating to personal relationships: 'really close to each other'; 'well-mannered and polite'; 'people sticking together'. Three referred to cultural aspects: 'famous buildings'; 'they don't wear dirty clothes'; 'they've kept up their traditions – old festivals and religion'. Three respondents gave examples of what they personally anticipated: 'want to go and meet people';

'they will treat us nicely ... they will want to be friendly'; 'they like to give gifts and have something in return.' One respondent's view was that people are 'encouraged to be involved in discussions about what's going on'.

Post-visit: Responses to the questions after the trip mostly reflected their personal experiences. Seven respondents referred to personal relationships and behaviour. The adjective 'friendly' was applied by the majority of them. Another observation made by two young people was that people helped and cared for each other. Four young people answered in a personal fashion about what they found good about the visit: 'we stayed for two days in a Russian family and they cared for us as their children, met a lot of new people and made friends'; 'going to see concerts, to bowls, Red Square and Lenin's tomb'; 'went to Red Square and learned about the war and Lenin'.

Only one respondent (the same number as pre-trip) mentioned political involvement: 'The kids were very aware of politics at a young age.' All the other good aspects referred to fell within the category of 'social fairness and distribution of wealth'. The proportion of young people mentioning this was unchanged.

The fact that people were trusted to pay the right fare on the buses was noted by two respondents. 'Everyone actually works' said one, while another remarked that they hadn't seen any tramps. However one respondent noted that 'some people were well off' and gave the example of Persian carpets being on the wall of the home she stayed in.

Responses to question: *What do you think the bad aspects are?*
Pre-visit: There was a variety of prior impressions as to what the bad aspects would be, although the greatest number (five) referred to expected political repression: 'There's a lot of police'; 'seen films where the KGB take people away'; 'security might be strict, tight, they don't even smile'; 'I think the public should have more freedom to do and say what they like, and be able to leave the country of their own free will'; 'no choice of parties'.

Two respondents referred to economic shortages: 'queuing for food'; 'deprivation'. Two believed that individual opportunities were restricted. Reluctance to voice stereotypes was expressed by two respondents and two said they did not know what the bad aspects were. One thought there were no bad aspects and one response focussed on nuclear issues: 'From what I see on TV and the media they have nuclear war and nuclear this and that and that's bad. I've heard they're trying to ban it.' One respondent expressed concern that the Soviets might complain about the group while they were there, and that there was a risk the group members would not respond properly in different situations.

Post-visit: A marked change in perception was revealed in the post-trip interviews. Five of the young people believed there to be no bad aspects. One reflected, 'There are too many people in London who live on the streets. I didn't see anybody sleeping on the streets there.' Of the others, six mentioned economic constraints: 'kids wearing the same thing for a week or two'; 'on the streets you see people selling stuff to earn money'; 'everything's expensive, except transport'; 'queues for food and little service'; 'although everyone has a home, some blocks are in bad condition'; 'lack of technology'; 'some shops are drab and it's old-fashioned but you would soon get used to it'. There were two interesting comments about social fairness (or lack of it): 'If you got brains you work for the government. If you got muscle you work for the people. If you work for the government, there's more money and higher standard of life'; 'Transport system is not accessible for people with disabilities.' This latter respondent also noted a 'lack of emphasis on individual creativity' and 'some sexism. Girls are treated differently.' She also noted that there were some 'touchy subjects for discussion' for example 'nuclear war'. The theme of political awareness and involvement was picked up by only one other respondent: 'military presence didn't help. It is not as bad as people think. All males do military service and at all times wear their uniform, therefore it looks like a large military presence.' Two respondents drew on their own experience of events and experiences to describe bad aspects: 'In the camp, the line-up was bad'; 'I didn't like road safety. Crossing is difficult and dangerous. I saw car accidents every day.'

Thus, the number of respondents referring to political repression fell from five pre-trip to two post-trip, while impressions of economic shortages were prominent, six as opposed to two pre-trip felt there were no bad aspects.

Responses to question: *What do you think the easier things would be for a girl/boy like you growing up in Moscow compared with Hackney?*
This particular question asks for responses based on the young people's reflection on their own experience of growing up within their particular culture. The young people in the pilot study shared a different culture in that they were all girls aged 15 to 17, all

white, and in or intending to go into sixth form. Not surprisingly
the coding categories developed from the pilot study were not
meaningful for grouping these young people's responses (see
concluding Note).

Pre-visit: Five participants said they did not know or did not think
it would be easier. The other comments mostly reflect the participants' experience of aspects of their life in Hackney. The most
frequent comments were about imagining it would be less violent
(three) and more disciplined (three): 'Not so much trouble there
between police and fights and all that'; 'Most people here are wild
and crazy – there's fights and beating up people. Over there there'll
be more discipline'; 'There'll be more discipline. They always obey
there. In Hackney they are often stubborn.' A 13 year-old girl
comments: 'maybe Russian people won't use "nick-names", they
won't say you're Turkish. Schools are nice there and life is
peaceful.' A 15 year-old girl thought an easier thing might be more
political involvement: 'more opportunity for kids in Moscow to
speak, although there's no guarantee they'll be listened to. In
Hackney, ILEA's "pupil parliament" was only to humour kids.'

Post-visit: Ten of the eleven participants offered a view of what they
thought the easier things would be. Nine of them were different
from their pre-visit comments. The child who pre-visit hoped they
would not use nick-names expressed similar views about racism but
this was expressed within a political context post-visit. 'It's much
better thinking socialist – it's fairer. They're not saying you're black
– it's bad, and you're white, it's good. They're not saying you're
Kurdish, it's bad.' Two participants commented about feeling safer
there. A 15 year-old girl commented 'the streets feel safer there.
There was no hassle in the streets.' Two girls welcomed the lack of
commercial pressure: 'There's less talk about possessions and material things. Everyone seemed to see each other as equal, and all
mucked in together.' 'It's easier to concentrate on school work.
There's more distractions here.' Another participant also thought it
would be easier to study there: 'They have more chance to study.
There are less choices in my school this year because we need the
money, but there's no problems like that there.'

Responses to question: *What do you think the harder things would be
for a girl/boy like you growing up in Moscow compared with Hackney?*
Pre-visit: Four participants said they did not know. The most
frequent comments were about restrictions (three): 'You wouldn't
be as free as you are in England to do whatever you want, for

example going out so much and coming back at night'; 'don't think they'd have freedom or independence like kids nowadays in Hackney, for example travelling on your own and speaking your own mind'; 'not so much choice in playing games and in what there is to eat. They wouldn't have much choice to run around when they like.' Two girls made comments reflecting their view that sexism there would make life harder: 'girls do sewing and cooking and men go out to work. It's old-fashioned'; 'girls are disadvantaged.' One boy felt the harder thing would be 'being taught to be a communist'.

Post-visit: Following their visit 10 of the 12 participants offered a view of what they thought the harder things would be. Eight of these were different from their pre-visit views. Three thought restrictions would make it harder, two of which were to do with restrictions on travel: 'not so easy to see the world and get experience of other countries.' One boy commented 'they are not allowed to wander out of Moscow with Moscow number plates. Even in the camp we had to obey rules, for example we have to be quiet after lunch.' Two thought education would be harder: 'not many computers in schools in Russia, and not as much sport'; 'Education seems old-fashioned. They don't even do drama.' Two thought restrictions on consumer goods would make it harder: 'harder to have a varied diet'; 'harder to buy things and do things.' One girl commented that it's harder to be a woman there: 'Some women do men's jobs. Some work as guards in museums. Some young women drive buses. We saw old women selling in markets, they have to work to support themselves. Some of them live on their own. It's hard for old women.'

Responses to question: *In what way do you think your ideas or images of the Soviet Union have changed?*

One said it was much as he expected and one had no preconceived impression. Ten of the 12 young people did state their changed ideas and images. Six commented that the Soviet people were friendlier than expected and two mentioned they were much friendlier than people in this country. A 13 year-old girl commented 'English and Russians are very different. In Russia all children treat all people like friends, but English children don't. You need to talk a lot to an English child to be a friend.' A 15 year-old described a range of changed ideas as a consequence of her visit: 'I was expecting more police and army round all of Moscow, I was expecting people to be quite cold. But they're not. They're very caring and friendly. It's a very beautiful city, with trees, not like London, where you hardly ever see a tree. I expected it to be dirtier, like London. It's not, I expected the streets to be very quiet, but it's very busy – it even has 10-lane streets.' Four commented on aspects of the architecture, for example they were surprised to see tower blocks and office blocks.

Personal Hopes and Fears

Responses to questions: *Can you think now about your life and future in general. What three things do you hope for most?* and *What three things are you most afraid of?*

These questions were previously used in a study of the attitudes of Finnish school children by Solantaus.[89] She used nine categories to code the responses. In the pilot study the responses were coded into those categories but the 'other' category was broken down into three new categories: 'Political factors in the UK', 'own death', and 'personal fulfilment'. Solantaus checked and agreed with our categorisations for this pilot study.

Using this system for the Hackney responses a significant number of responses (five) fell outside these categories (except the 'other' category). We therefore made a new category: 'travel-related hopes and fears' to account for the majority of responses in this section.

Hopes and Fears – Those Mentioned First

Pre-visit: The number of responses was too small to justify the use of percentages for analysis but percentages are given for comparative purposes with other studies. No one fear predominated over others. Fear of failing school exams was the commonest fear (three participants). Two fourth-year and one fifth-year interviewee expressed this fear, for example 'failing my exams'; 'all I think about is work in school and the exams.' The second most common first fears were those concerning health of family and friends (two participants), for example 'losing my parents'; 'death – my own and my family's'; and fears relating to money, for example 'not having no money'. Only one participant, a 12 year-old, expressed fear of war as a first fear: 'the bomb dropping. There have been prophecies of World War III with nasty images – eyes fall out of your head and your skin falls off.'

The first most common hopes were those to do with work and employment. Five participants expressed this hope, for example 'a good job working in an office'; 'have a good job, for example computer programmer, translator, solicitor'; 'to have a job – like a car designer'; 'a job that I'm happy in'. The next commonest first hope was to do with travel (three participants), for example 'to get a picture of the world and peoples' lives'; 'to visit America to compare it with Russia'; 'travel the world'.

Post-visit: Four participants gave different first fears after their trip. One more participant, a boy, rated World War III as his first fear. A 15 year-old girl's first fear was 'not being able to go back to Russia if my Mum said "no" – but I'd still go.'

Seven participants gave different first hopes after their trip. Of these, three of them had travel hopes: 'hope to travel and make friends in different countries and keep in touch when I go back'; 'to go and live in the Soviet Union'; and 'to go back to Turkey because we can't now because we're communist'. One 12 year-old boy changed his first hope to 'peace'.

Distribution of all hopes and fears (regardless of order)
Participants were not asked to prioritise or rank their hopes and fears. (If a participant expressed more than one hope or fear in the same category it was only recorded once.)

Pre-visit: Fear of death or ill-health for parents or family members was the commonest fear. Four participants had this as one of their three worries, for example 'grandparents dying – they give me advice'; 'If my parents don't get better.' Fear of war was an equal second most common fear (three participants) along with employment fears and fears for one's own health. Two of the three participants with health fears were boys with particular worries about AIDS. One boy's anxiety may have been exacerbated by misinformation: 'I'm afraid of diseases, cancer or AIDS. You get diseases through dishes and plates. I'm worried for myself and my family.'

Knowledge of Soviet Involvement in Second World War
In the pre-trip interviews only five of the 12 young people knew which side the Soviets were on. Two pupils did not know there had been a large war called the Second World War. Four young people gained knowledge during their visit particularly on the extent of the Soviet involvement in the war: 'They lost a lot of people. We went to the museums'; 'They lost a quarter of their population. They lost more lives than the English.' However there was some confusion for some of them. A 15 year-old boy, in response to 'what do you know of the effect of the war on that country?'

replied: 'A lot. It made them turn against the Czar and things. It made them communist. Twenty million died.'

Overall knowledge of Soviet involvement in the Second World War was quite limited before the visit and not changed substantially by the visit.

Attitudes Towards International Relations Including Nuclear Policy

Responses to questions: *Do you think we need to be afraid of the Soviet Union? Do you think we need nuclear weapons because of a threat from the Soviet Union? Are there other reasons why you think we need nuclear weapons?*

Eleven of the 12 young people did not believe the Soviet Union to be a threat before the visit. 'If the Soviet Union was a threat we wouldn't have been allowed to go over there.' The other one was uncertain and his uncertainty persisted. Three participants did think Britain needed nuclear weapons and this view also persisted. Most of the young people voiced strong views about the danger and wasted money of having nuclear weapons. As the 15 year-old commented 'We don't need them. There is no threat. We have them for Mrs Thatcher's pride' and 'A waste of money and life.' A 12 year-old commented 'I think the government wants them because they're afraid of the Soviet Union and don't trust the Soviet Union. But I don't think that. If we got rid of them, all the other countries will follow in pursuit.'

The commonest view of the young people who did think we needed nuclear weapons is reflected in this 14 year-old's response: 'We shouldn't be afraid of the Soviet Union. We need nuclear weapons because some countries might take us over if we didn't have them.'

Thus these three held a strong view about the need for a nuclear deterrent independent of having a belief about a Soviet threat and this view was not changed by their visit.

Responses to question: *Have you got any ideas that could improve relations between this country and the Soviet Union?*

Pre-visit: Nine of the 12 interviewees did have ideas before their visit. Five of these were ideas about enabling more ordinary people to visit each other's countries, for example 'more travelling prospects, children coming and going, coming to schools, to see how their country differs from the other.' Three felt government leaders could do more, for example, 'They could make an arrangement between Thatcher and Gorbachev not to use nuclear weapons against England.' 'The two leaders should get together more often on a socialising basis not just ordinary meetings.' Two felt political change was needed in this country: 'a Labour government'; 'Have a new government, but not Labour as Kinnock wants Trident. It might be a dream, but the Green Party in a few generations.'

Post-visit: Eleven of the twelve interviewees had ideas to improve relations between the two countries after their visit. The ideas of one 13 year-old boy, who said he didn't know how to improve relations prior to the visit, implied the effects the visit had on him: 'If we want to be friends with the Soviet Union we must learn their language or they must learn ours. We must be friends with them. If someone says "Let's do this" then they must decide together. They must have a dialogue to decide together.' A 14 year-old boy who said he didn't know before the visit suggested relations could only be improved by 'getting rid of Thatcher's government'.

After their visit three of the young people felt exchange visits could do much to improve relations (for example 'more things like twinning but on a larger scale, this way people are not so ignorant of each other'; 'In the long run exchanges will help people to see people for what they are not just the biased stuff on the telly').

Discussion

All twelve young people said they really enjoyed their visit and most expressed a desire to return. Most expressed a warm liking for the Soviet youngsters they were in contact with at the pioneer camp, and many developed friendships which they hoped to maintain by correspondence. This positive experience affected their attitudes and images. Six thought the Soviet people were friendlier than expected and two mentioned that they were friendlier than people over here.

Before the visit the aspects of Soviet society perceived as good most often were to do with social fairness ('there are not very rich and poor people') and this view was reinforced by their experiences during their visit ('no tramps or people having to sleep on the streets').

Favourable attitudes about social fairness were commented on, for example being trusted to pay the fare on buses, and lack of commercial pressure. However, some participants expressed disappointment that some people obviously had considerably more privileges than others. This was reinforced by noting that the families who were their hosts for the last two days were considerably more affluent than the children they had been with at the pioneer camp. Girls also commented that sexism would make it harder for them ('girls are disadvantaged. They do the sewing and cooking. It's old-fashioned'). Their experiences changed their views of the bad aspects of Soviet society. Worries of political repression predominated before their visit. After the visit this was not commented on; instead there was a developing awareness of constraints in consumer goods and range of activities these young people were used to.

Attitudes and images were rarely expressed using societal or political concepts but rather in terms of their own social experience in the Soviet Union. It seems their changed attitudes and ideas directly related to their experience of being with Soviet people and in the families. One youngster remarked, 'We didn't meet enough people to get an impression (about the lack of things we take for granted here). We only really met the kids at the camp and the family.' Experience with a broader cross-section of Soviet society may have enabled the young people to develop ideas about political and broader societal issues.

There was scant knowledge of Soviet involvement in the Second World War and this was not changed substantially by the visit. It may be that visits to museums need to be backed up by discussion to enable young people to understand key aspects of Soviet history. There was no mention of glasnost or perestroika. There was some confusion about what communism was about. One 15 year-old considered that a bad aspect of Soviet society was 'communism', and a good aspect the fact the society 'shares the money it makes, and people work together properly'.

Favourable attitudes were anticipated and experienced in contrast to their own experiences in inner-city London. Of particular note were attitudes about violence and personal safety. The six young people who hoped Soviet society would be less violent and more orderly were from black or ethnic minority communities, which may well reflect their particular negative experience of being black in an inner city. Several girls, though noting aspects of sexism in education and domestic life, commented favourably that in the Soviet Union the streets felt safer, and there was 'no hassle on the streets'.

Hopes and fears of the Hackney young people show interesting similarities and differences from those described in other studies. Fear of death or ill-health of parents and fear of failing school exams were the most commonly held fears of the Hackney young people. The fear of death of parents is a commonly expressed fear of young people in many previous studies from North America and Europe. In a study in Southern California[43] it was the commonest fear followed by school performance then nuclear war. The Hackney youngsters were different in that relatively few mentioned war as one of their fears.

Only one Hackney youngster mentioned fear of war as a first fear pre-visit, whereas in Solantaus's study[89] 79 per cent of the Finnish 12 year-olds and 48 per cent of 18 year-olds mentioned the possibility of war as their first fear. Three Hackney young people (25 per cent) mentioned war as one of their three fears. In the Finnish study 81 per cent listed fear of war as one of their three fears and in a similar study in Canada[90] 51 per cent named war and peace as one of their three major worries. In our pilot study approximately 75 per cent of the 15 to 17 year-old girls expressed fear of war as one of their three fears.

It is interesting to consider the differing contexts and the salience of the threat of war in relation to other threatening events in these young people's lives to help understand these differences[94] although the numbers in this study mean this is purely speculative. First, the research studies quoted were conducted at a time of much greater international tension whereas this exchange took place in the Gorbachev era within a political context of increasing international cooperation and general perception of lessening of any Soviet threat. Secondly, the Hackney young people were subject to inner-city stresses and had realistic immediate anxieties about their personal security in terms of secure employment and emotional and perhaps economic dependence on their family. These may have outweighed the seemingly more remote threat of nuclear war. In contrast the girls in the pilot study were not subject to these socio-economic pressures and were realistically confident about obtaining educational qualifications and secure employment. Thirdly, the fact that the *Daily Mirror* was the most frequently read paper in the Hackney youngsters' households compared to the *Guardian* and *Independent* in the pilot study girls' households is likely to relate to differences in the extent and nature of discussions in the home about nuclear and international issues. This is not to say the Hackney young people were politically unsophisticated. Two of them expressed their fear in relation to political forces in this country: 'that progress in society is being and will be reversed'; 'Margaret Thatcher getting into power again'.

Alternatively, there may have been ignorance about the issue. It would have been interesting to ask a question about their expecta-

tion of a nuclear war happening in their lifetime to further eluci-
date the issue.

Travel-related hopes and fears were commonly expressed, unlike
in other studies. Possibly this reflected the multi-cultural nature of
the group, for example with a Turkish child with a parent from the
Caribbean either fearing they would have to go back if a relative
died or wanting to travel to Jamaica. The excited anticipations
before going to the Soviet Union may well have generated more
hopes for travel. Certainly the experience of being there seemed to
broaden many of the young people's perspectives about the world
and their own part in it, and the overall number of fears expressed
was less after the visit. One participant, a 15 year-old girl, had
never been away from home before, let alone abroad or on an aeroplane. Her hopes before and after the visit reflect this shift. Before
the visit her hopes were to 'stay honest, carry on being friendly and
make my family happy and proud of me if I do the right thing'.
After the visit her hopes were to 'travel and make friends in
different countries and keep in touch when I get back, have fun
and be happy'.

The visit did not change the youngsters' view of the Soviet
Union as a threat, as 11 of the 12 did not believe it to be a threat
before the visit. The other one was uncertain and his uncertainty
persisted. Three participants did think Britain needed nuclear
weapons. They did not see the Soviet Union as a threat, however,
but felt the weapons were needed to deter unspecified other countries from invading. The majority, however, held very strong views
about the danger and waste of money and human life in having
nuclear weapons.

Eleven of the 12 interviewees had ideas to improve relations
between the two countries after their visit. These were mostly to do
with people from the two countries getting to know each other
better, both at government level and suggesting more exchange
visits of ordinary people.

It seems the kind of contact the young people had with the
Soviet youngsters enabled them to appreciate the common
humanity and friendliness of the Soviet people and to acknowledge
and be interested in the differences. Their comments and ideas to
improve relations between the two countries reflected hopes that
they can be part of this process: 'If more people went and got to see
the country and meet the people and come back and tell people,
people would not be so ignorant and frightened. We're young, we
can influence the younger generation.'

A Visit-leader's Perspective on the Exchange and Formal Evaluation

I (A.W.) am a Russian speaker who has worked in the USSR. I have a background in social work and counselling. My co-leader was an experienced teacher who stepped in at short notice to replace another teacher halfway through the preparation process and has a broad interest in international links. I have written this report with the aim of contributing to the development of good practice with regard to East–West exchange. I have particularly focussed on setting objectives, preparatory meetings, issues for leaders, the difficulties and challenges encountered and our attempts at dealing with them.

Shortly before going we drew up a list of possible measures of success. This included: good communication between the two of us, between ourselves and the young people, within the Hackney group as a whole and between us and the Soviets; Soviet and Hackney young people spending time together and their contacts enduring afterwards; young people taking the initiative and finding productive solutions to difficulties; young people being actively curious, understanding that societies have good and bad aspects to them, having open political perspectives, developing a culture of respect for ourselves and others; having group meetings, possibly daily, to air gripes and find solutions.

My main interest was in supporting the young people to make real relationships with each other, by interpreting for them when necessary and providing information and opportunities to think about cultural differences.

In preparatory sessions we asked the young people to focus on what they were expecting to be different and how the Soviets might find us different; what we might bring to the USSR to demonstrate our different cultures – songs, dances, etc; how we should deal with economic and material difference – what we should bring with us and what we should leave behind; what being a 'diplomat' means and where it might get tricky. We made up ice-breaking games in Russian and organised a sponsored Russian language 'learn-in'. We also invited a black youth worker with experience of the USSR to talk to the young people and their parents about what it is like for a black person visiting the Soviet Union – that they were likely to meet much unconcealed curiosity but unlikely to meet hostility. (My co-leader and I are both white and were able to work unpaid. A black youth-worker we had attempted to recruit was unable to get the secondment she needed.)

At the pioneer camp initially we continued to hold regular group meetings. One session was particularly useful. Each person wrote down a fear they were experiencing, placed it in a hat, and we read them out and discussed them anonymously. However the meetings reminded the young people of school and consumed time that they wanted to spend with their new Soviet friends; we abandoned them.

There were several factors that made it more or less possible to achieve our aims, and which we attempted to develop an understanding of during the course of the trip.

Perhaps the most significant was the naturalness of the welcome, warmth and interest expressed by the camp's residents. The younger Russians particularly seemed to operate from an assumption of physical closeness and warmth, completely ignored the British young people's reserve and would pull me in to interpret for them. The formal evaluation picks up the extent to which the Hackney young people were struck by the Soviets' friendliness but misses the ways their behaviour changed. The effect on the group as a whole was striking. It became acceptable for them to be far more affectionate to each other than they were used to being in London. I took many slides of the Hackney young people with their arms around each other and their young Soviet friends. Back in London they were extremely embarrassed to see those pictures. Several of the young people took significant personal steps forward. Many took risks with performing that they said they would not have imagined taking before. Others who were initially painfully reserved came out of themselves. I talked to the mother of one intensely shy and tense young man on our return. She said that he had changed beyond all belief, that he had come home and cried solidly at losing his new friends, having never wept before, and for the first time was taking the initiative in contacting and seeing people in London instead of staying on his own at home. Many of the young people formed relationships that really mattered to them and learnt a great deal in the process.

The formal evaluation reflects the young people's positive impressions of the Soviet accent on collectivism and cooperation, and it may have been that these stimulated the development of cooperation within the Hackney group. Several of the young people commented on leaving how much they liked the way they came to sort things out within the group. Keen to work without adult intervention, they prepared several dances to present at a concert on different ethnic themes. These were particularly striking, not just for their inclusiveness but for the way they gave a central place to two young people who had a tendency to be scapegoated. They were extremely thoughtful about race issues, presenting us with a means for allocating young people to host families for the last few days so that each black young person would be accompanied by a white ally.

The Soviets do not share our concept of privacy or our sense of the need for it. The young people adapted quickly to the fact that they would never be on their own rather more quickly than we did as adults. We adults began to see how essential it was for the two of us to take time to support each other in adjusting to cultural differences.

Although we lived in close proximity with the Soviets, there were some things that kept us separate. We tended to be treated as guests of honour, there were not the same expectations of us as of the young Soviets and we were not involved in the running of the camp. The most difficult aspect of this was that we as visitors were served better food. There was also a strong emphasis on entertaining us. Every third day or so we were taken as a group on sightseeing excursions to Moscow.

The young people certainly enjoyed these aspects enormously and it may be that they gained something on a deeper level from their 'royal' treatment. However, I think that this made it less possible for them to see the country through the eyes of their young friends. But it cannot be good for the young Soviets to see our young people receiving preferential treatment; this could have an adverse effect on their relationships.

The evaluation reflects the way the Hackney young people wrestled with issues of economic and material difference throughout the trip. The Russian young people were grateful merely for a chance to examine our cassette players and computer games. Some of the Hackney young people began to notice the way they took their possessions for granted and to appreciate that the material difference must have affected the Russian young people, though not all of them were free enough of their own feelings of deprivation to be able to think well about the young Russians in this area.

Hackney and Krasnaya Presnya are committed to 'the establishment of friendly, constructive relations between appropriate citizens and community groups', but given the cost of communications there is little opportunity for prior discussion of what would best bring these about. The summer camp is wholly separate from Krasnaya Presnya district and staff are seconded from work organisations for the summer period only. We were somewhat timid in requesting that we be more fully incorporated into the life of the camp and could have been much more active in consulting with the camp staff and the Krasnaya Presnya administration over our activities.

Much of the time at the camp was spent in unstructured ways. Many found that they could build up relationships during this time, but others might have benefited from more joint structured activities. Many of the young Soviets spoke some English, but we would have done well to develop enjoyable ways for the young people to learn from each other.

The evaluation gives useful feedback on the lack of substantial improvement in the young people's knowledge of Soviet involvement in the Second World War and the confusion some of them experienced over communism. We visited parts of the Museum of Krasnaya Presnya devoted to the 1905–6 revolution, the section of the Museum of the Soviet Army devoted to the Second World War, the Tomb of the Unknown Soldier and the Lenin Mausoleum. I think the young people found it hard to relate to this information in the way it was presented, particularly when listening to it through an interpreter. Additionally our own feelings about the war and differences in our two approaches may have meant that we did not set up a sufficiently supportive environment to discuss the war. Looking at the evaluation I wondered if there might be a relationship between the young people's difficulty in acquiring information about the war and the absence noted in the evaluation of war as a fear.

My guess is that, if anything, difficulties we had in setting up a relaxed learning environment and that we had not set up a prior expectation of learning were more likely to be the reasons for the young people not developing 'ideas about political and broader social issues', rather than because they met an insufficiently broad cross-section of Soviet people. In fact I was struck by the mixed range of young people at the camp, children from ordinary Moscow workers' families as well as the child of an astronaut and senior politician.

To what extent did we achieve our goals? Many of the young people established real relationships with young people with whom they are continuing to correspond. Several are considering inviting them to visit. I think it is essential not to undervalue this. The trip made a major personal difference to most of them. The majority became more outgoing and acquired a stronger sense of their importance in the world. This was not a school trip but a trip to a summer camp, and we did not set a prior expectation that learning about the Soviet Union and its history would be a feature. It might have been useful to have done this and to have set up joint learning activities with the young Soviets. However, many returned with a strong motivation to learn more. On their request I set up a weekly Russian-language-for-beginners adult education class for six of the young people, two siblings and three parents. All attend regularly and use the class as a focus for continued activities. Interestingly, the formal evaluation may itself have prompted several of the young people to think more about their experience. Three wrote long descriptions of the trip for display purposes, basing their thoughts around many of the questions asked in their interviews.

Conclusions

These concluding comments aim to make a contribution towards the development of good practice for East–West youth exchanges and are based on what has been learnt from the evaluation of this particular visit. The attitudes of the young people described here cannot be taken as representative of young people in the UK as these Hackney youngsters are atypical in many ways. But what can be emphasised is that these young people, in the age range 12–15 years who did not know each other before, coming from diverse cultural backgrounds, different schools and educational levels, all enjoyed their visit. They were informed through their contacts with Soviet young people and many developed a broader perspective about the world and their part in it. Salient points are suggested to aid planning for exchange visits in ways that will structure appropriate opportunities for learning and enhance the support for the young people in their relationships with their peers from Eastern bloc countries. Points suggested are selection of participants and leaders, preparation, prior negotiations with the hosts, opportunities for personal contacts and learning during the visit, leaders' behaviour and attitudes, and evaluation.

Selection
Equal opportunities principles were applied to ensure the group had an equal representation of girls and boys and reflected the cultural diversity in this borough. The initial contacts through schools did not provide the cultural diversity and this was subsequently established through invitations to youth clubs and

community groups. This raises questions of how best to ensure that equal access to this opportunity is provided. It was hoped that joint responsibility for fundraising encouraged young people to take part whose parents may have been otherwise deterred by the costs involved. The diversity of the group enabled the Soviets to appreciate the diversity of young people in Britain and was perhaps a useful experience at this time in the USSR when ethnic and racial tensions are to the fore.

The leaders were selected, not on the basis of organising school trips, but for their experience of the Soviet Union and youth work. This was seen to be important as the aims for the leaders included supporting young people in their relationships with their Soviet counterparts and negotiating with their hosts. One leader was fluent in Russian which was a great advantage.

Preparation
The six pre-visit preparation meetings with leaders, participants and interested parents were most valuable in developing group cohesion, awareness of possible difficulties and reducing apprehensions. In retrospect, more information on salient aspects of Soviet history and politics may have given these young people a basis to acquire more knowledge during their visit.

Preliminary Negotiations with the Host
Our Soviet hosts treated the Hackney young people like honoured guests and this was much appreciated but led to a degree of segregation. The leaders would have liked to have been involved in the preliminary negotiations to see if there could be greater closeness. Suggestions would include asking for the young people to be incorporated into the work programmes in the camp and structuring more joint activities, games and projects. Difficulties and delays in communication mean negotiations need to start a long time in advance.

There is a prevailing view in this country that young people will get most out of an exchange visit if they stay with families. However, many young people who stay with families abroad become homesick and feel isolated. Unhappy young people are rarely curious or interested in developing new relationships. These young people spent most of their time in a young pioneer camp, the normal experience for Soviet youngsters in the summer months. Some of the young people were very homesick initially but were well supported through it by the leaders and their peers.

We are not adopting a rigid position about group versus home-stays but highlighting the need to think about various ways of supporting young people who become lonely or distressed.

Points for Leaders
Leaders carry considerable responsibility and it can be a stressful and exhausting experience. Our leaders found it necessary to spend time with each other to go over issues and work out ways to support each other. The evaluation indicated that the young people did not learn much about Soviet history and politics from museum visits. In retrospect the leaders felt they could have provided more opportunities for group discussion with the young people during the visit to help consolidate their experiences.

Evaluation
The evaluation of this exchange visit was formalised as a research study. To minimise bias, interviewers were used who were not taking part in the visit and different interviewers interviewed the participants before and after the visit. Less formal procedures may provide a richer source of material to aid understanding of the process of change, as a basis for improving future exchanges, and may help the young people to reflect more on their experiences. For example, the leaders may find it useful to interview the young people before and after the visit which would offer continuity to the young person and enable the leaders to make a relationship with each individual. Video recordings of changes in social relations taking place over the period would also have been very informative. However, the young people did find the pre- and post-interviews in this study useful to help orientate their thinking and reflect on their experience on their return. (Interest from Soviet researchers in collaborating on evaluating the effects of an exchange visit of Soviet youngsters to this country would be very welcome.)

Follow-up
All the Hackney young people were enthusiastic about their visit and it was useful to provide validating opportunities to talk about what they had learnt about the Soviet Union. Some were able to talk to newspaper and radio journalists and others had opportunities in youth clubs and schools. Some wanted to learn Russian as they were keen to return to the Soviet Union. Others wanted to be hosts to Soviet young people on a return exchange visit. There has

been an enthusiastic response to the leader's offer to run a weekly Russian class. This class also provides a continuing focus for discussion and learning about the Soviet Union.

The nature of exchanges differs. Some are developed through twinning arrangements between boroughs and cities, others through individual schools in the two countries developing links, and others through youth exchange programmes. Whatever the process it is hoped that increasing opportunities will be provided for young people from East and West to get to know each other, appreciate their common humanity and acknowledge and respect their differences.

Notes

Heather Hunt is a clinical psychologist, Michael Orgel a medical doctor and Lesley Morrison a community physician. All are employed within the NHS and involved with SPINA on a voluntary basis. Armorer Wason works in East–West exchange and was one of the leaders of the visit.

The interview protocols, tables of coding categories, and figures showing the young people's hopes and fears are available, on request, from the authors, c/o MCANW, 601 Holloway Road, London N19 4DJ.

Appendix II

Organisations Involved in USSR–UK Exchange

with special reference to young people's and non-governmental medical exchanges

Young people's exchanges are organised through twinning, individual ventures and through the recent initiative by Kenneth Baker, the UK Minister of Education. City twinning is one of the best-established opportunities for East–West exchange. Information on existing links and how to set up new twinning arrangements can be obtained from the Joint Twinning Committee of the Local Authorities Association of Great Britain (10 Spring Gardens, London W1; tel. 01 930 8466). One of the most active and successful of the established links is Sheffield/Donetsk (contact Liz Howarth or Jim Coleman, Town Hall, Sheffield; tel. 0742 72644). Sheffield hosted the biannual UK–USSR twinning conference in July 1989.

The Society for Cultural Relations, 320 Brixton Road, London SW9 (tel. 01 274 2282) brings young Soviet people together with their British counterparts each year. In 1989 the young people were jointly involved in ecological and environmental projects. The Society has names of Soviet medical personnel keen to meet their British counterparts and health service workers to promote exchange.

The Youth Exchange Centre, Seymour Mews House, London W1H 9PE (tel. 01 486 5101) provides guidelines and some financial support for people seeking to organise exchanges.

The Central Bureau for Educational Visits and Exchanges (same address as Youth Exchange Centre above) administers the newly-launched programme of school-to-school partnerships. Schools (not individuals) may apply, although there is already a long waiting list.

The UK–USSR Medical Exchange Programme (480 Banbury Road, Oxford; Hon. Sec. Stewart Britten, 9d Stanhope Road, London N6 5NE; tel. 01 348 1795) promotes exchanges for people in the medical field. They have organised a study tour for workers in primary healthcare for 1990.

The GB–USSR Association (14 Grosvenor Place, London SW1;

tel. 01 235 2116) is another useful organisation.

The International Council for New Initiatives in East–West Co-operation, based in Vienna, organised an *International Conference on East–West Co-operation and Health Issues: Challenges for the Year 2000*, at the Royal College of Physicians in October 1989.

Interchange (27 Stafford Road, Croydon, Surrey CR0 4NG; tel. 01 681 3612) organises visits for specialist groups – GPs, dentists, physiotherapists, child psychologists, etc.

Citizen's Diplomacy: A Handbook on Anglo–Soviet Initiatives (Merlin Press Ltd, 10 Malden Road, London NW5 3HR) dates from 1986 but is still useful.

It has become much simpler to invite Soviet citizens to the UK. A letter of invitation, stating that all expenses in the UK will be paid by the host, and signed by a solicitor, is all that is needed. It is essential to contact the Home Office first for full details (Lunar House, Wellesley Road, Croydon CR9 2BY; tel. 01 686 0688).

Appendix III
Psychodynamic Empowerment

Several workshops took place during MCANW's Conference *The Nuclear Mentality – Dynamics and Change* on which this publication is based. One of the workshops was entitled 'Psychodynamic Empowerment' and initiated by the British group Psychotherapists Against Nuclear Disaster (PAND).

This group exists to study the emotions aroused in individuals by the nuclear threat and the ways in which groups, including families, become involved in assumptions current in their social systems about war and defences against conflict. Two members of PAND comment on this work and the Conference workshop:

From the workshop and our experience of other conferences on the nuclear question we saw that conference participants welcome an opportunity to talk about personal responses. This is an area where psychoanalytic insight is useful since groups of this kind are an everyday part of the psychotherapy and counselling world, whereas for many people places for personal discussion with like-minded others are not easy to find. The topics of helplessness and how to become effective in the face of the overwhelming nuclear threat are particularly important. However, we wondered if the opportunity we could provide at this conference might be too minimal.

There was pressure from some in the group to be in smaller groups. We thought that in a conference entitled *Dynamics and Change*, with a strong psychoanalytic contribution, we might have used our desire to empower ourselves by firmly suggesting a section for small discussion groups at which more participants could share feelings and insights after the rich input from speakers.

However, within our actual time constraint of one and a half hours we had deliberately chosen to have two conductors and a larger group; small enough for some sense of personal meeting but big enough to mirror the possibility of moving from the sense of impossibility and impersonality in large numbers to a sense of personal effectiveness. In effect, our 'boundary' problems did symbolise both international problems of language (actual, conceptual and descriptive) and the tension between action and reflection when conflict and fear threaten from within and without.

The input of the conference had stirred the desire to act, to know, and to know what to do. The workshop demonstrated the necessity, in order to arrive at purposeful action, of thinking reflectively about what is known and what is stirred up (such as fear, paranoia, helplessness, the desire for facts) in circumstances where group pressures demand collective conformity and the individual feels unable to use his or her own insights.

Psychotherapists Against Nuclear Disaster (PAND)

This is a network of psychotherapists working in a variety of settings, who look at issues connected with nuclear warfare and nuclear power within a framework of analytical psychotherapy. We feel we have a duty to heighten our awareness of our response to these overwhelming issues. We also have a responsibility to promote greater awareness of society's response, particularly in its unconscious aspects.

Members of PAND offer professional insights into the prevention of nuclear disaster and the effects of living under the threat of nuclear war, and may be able to use professional experience to unblock the log-jam of accusation and counter-accusation that often characterises the nuclear debate.

The organisation was formed in 1985 by a small group of psychotherapists. The main organisation, known to members as 'the umbrella organisation', meets approximately every two months for Saturday workshops set around a topic with introductory speakers, small groups and a plenary meeting. From this main organisation have grown a number of small groups, each developing individually but with the aim of supporting members as they struggle to address their feelings about the possibility of nuclear war. The local groups usually meet once a month.

The aims of the PAND network are:

- To explore and share feelings and knowledge about nuclear issues: how they affect us, our patients or clients, and public attitudes. This is done amongst ourselves by circulating reading lists, inviting speakers and conducting discussions.
- To take action as thought appropriate, which might entail: political involvement, making links with MPs, liaising and

running workshops with other groups similarly concerned, transmitting our knowledge and awareness to other people and generally making a contribution towards the prevention of nuclear war.

Further information may be obtained from the Secretary, 58 Roupell Street, London SE1.

References

1. Allison, Graham T. *Essence of Decision: Explaining the Cuban Missile Crisis* (Boston: Little, Brown, 1971).
2. Alloy, L.B. *et al.*, 'The Hopelessness Theory of Depression: Attributional Aspects', *British Journal of Clinical Psychology*, 1988, vol. 27, pp. 5–21.
3. Axelrod, R. (ed.) *Structure of Decision* (Princeton: Princeton University Press, 1976).
4. Axelrod, R. *The Evolution of Cooperation* (New York: Basic Books, 1984).
5. Barash, D. *The Arms Race and Nuclear War* (Belmont, California: Wadsworth, 1987).
6. Bennett, P. G. and Dando, M. R. 'The Arms Race: Is It Just a Mistake?', *New Scientist*, 1983, vol. 97, no. 1345, pp. 432–5.
7. Berkowitz, L. and Le Page, A. 'How Guns Control Us', *Psychology Today*, 1981, vol. 15, no. 6, pp. 11–12.
8. Bion, W. 'Group Dynamics: A Review', in Klein, M., Heimann, P., and MoneyKyrle, R. (eds) *New Directions in Psycho-analysis* (London: Tavistock, 1955).
9. Bowlby, John, 'Dr John Bowlby at 80 Talks to Anne Shearer', *Guardian*, 10 March 1989.
10. Britten, S. *The Invisible Event* (London: Menard, 1983).
11. Brook-Shepherd, G. *Storm Birds: Soviet Postwar Defectors* (London: Weidenfeld & Nicolson, 1988).
12. Burke, Patrick, *The Nuclear Weapons World* (London: Pinter, 1988).
13. Canadian Institute for International Peace and Security 'The Superpowers and International Security: Results of a 3-Country Comparative Survey', *Peace and Security*, 1988/9, vol. 3, no. 4.
14. Chalupa, General Leopold, 'The Defence of Central Europe: Implications of Change', *Journal of the Royal United Services Institute for Defence Studies*, March 1985, pp. 13–17.
15. Cohn, Carol, 'Sex and Death in the Rational World of Defense Intellectuals', *Signs: Journal of Women in Culture and Society*, 1987, vol. 12, no. 4, pp. 687–718.

16. Coyne, J. C. *et al.* 'The Role of Cognition in Depression: A Critical Appraisal', *Psychological Bulletin*, 1983, vol. 94, pp. 472–505.

17. Davies, R. *Children's Conceptualisations of the Threat from Nuclear Weapons* (Lancaster: Richardson Institute for Conflict and Peace Research, University of Lancaster, 1986).

18. ——. *Hopes and Fears: Children's Attitudes to Nuclear War*, Occasional Paper No. 2 (Lancaster: Centre for Peace Studies, St Martin's College, 1987).

19. Deutsch, M. 'Strategies of Inducing Cooperation', in White, R.K. (ed.) *Psychology and the Prevention of Nuclear War* (New York: New York University Press, 1986).

20. Dixon, Norman F. *On the Psychology of Military Incompetence* (London: Cape, 1976).

21. ——. *Our Own Worst Enemy* (London: Cape, 1987).

22. Douglas, M. *Risk Acceptability According to the Social Sciences* (London: Routledge & Kegan Paul, 1986).

23. Dyer, J. 'What Children Know and Feel about Nuclear War: Evidence from Research', *Scottish Educational Review*, 21, 1, pp. 36–47, 1989.

24. Eden, Colin, Jones, Sue and Sims, David, *Thinking in Organisations* (Basingstoke: Macmillan, 1979).

25. Eldridge, John, 'Public Opinion and the Media', in Davis, Howard, *Ethics and Defence* (Oxford: Blackwell, 1986).

26. Elworthy, S. *How Nuclear Weapons Decisions Are Made* (Basingstoke: Macmillan, 1986).

27. ——. *Who Decides? Accountability and Nuclear Weapons Decision-Making in Britain* (Oxford: Oxford Research Group, 1987).

28. Erikson, E.H. 'Eight Ages of Man', in *Childhood and Society* (New York: Norton, 1963).

29. Escalona, S.K. 'Children's Awareness of the Threat of War: Some Developmental Implications', *American Journal of Orthopsychiatry*, 1963, vol. 33, pp. 204–5.

30. European Commission, *Caring For Children*, Report of the European Commission's Child Care Network (London: EC, 1988).

31. Fairhall, David, 'Black and Decker Allies', *Guardian*, 23 October 1987.

32. Fenton, I. (ed.) *The Psychology of Nuclear Conflict* (London: Coventure, 1986).

33. Fischhoff, B. *et al. Acceptable Risk* (London: Cambridge University Press, 1984).

34. Flynn, G. and Rattinger, H. (eds.) *The Public and Atlantic Defense* (London: Croom Helm, 1985).

35. Frank, J.D. 'Pre-Nuclear Age Leaders and the Nuclear Arms Race', in Fenton, I. (ed.) *The Psychology of Nuclear Conflict* (London: Coventure, 1986).

36. Frei, D. *Risks of Unintentional Nuclear War* (London: Croom Helm, 1983).

37. Friedman, B. 'Preschoolers' Awareness of the Nuclear Threat' CA Assoc. Educ. Young Children, *Newsletter*, 1984, vol. 12, pp. 4–5.

38. Gillies, P., Ellwood, J.M., Hawtin, P. and Ledwith, F. 'Anxieties in Adolescents about Unemployment and War', *British Medical Journal*, 1985, vol. 291, pp. 145–51.

39. Glasgow Media Group, *War and Peace News*, p. 260 (Oxford: Oxford University Press, 1985).

40. Glover, E. *War, Sadism and Pacifism* (London: Allen & Unwin, 1946).

41. Goldberg, S. *et al.*, 'Thinking about the Threat of Nuclear War: Relevance to Mental Health', *American Journal of Orthopsychiatry*, 1985, vol. 55, no. 4, p. 503.

42. Goldman, D.S. and Greenberg, W.M. 'Preparing for Nuclear War. The Psychological Effects', *American Journal of Psychiatry*, 1982, vol. 52, no. 4, pp. 580–1.

43. Goldenring, J.M. and Doctor, R. 'Teenage Worry about Nuclear War: North American and European Questionnaire Studies', in Schwebel, M. (ed.) 'Mental Health Implications of Life in the Nuclear Age', *International Journal of Mental Health*, 1986, vol. 15, pp. 72–92.

44. ———. 'Use and Threat of Nuclear Weapons', *Lancet*, 12 November 1988, p. 1140.

45. Greenwald, David S. and Zeitlin, Steven J. *No Reason to Talk about It: Families Confront the Nuclear Threat* (New York: Norton, 1987).

46. Gromyko, Anatoli and Helman, Martin (eds.) *Breakthrough: Emerging New Thinking. Soviet and Western Scholars Issue a Challenge to Build a World Beyond War* (New York: Walker, 1988) p. 85.

47. Halperin, Morton H. *Bureaucratic Politics and Foreign Policy* (Washington DC: Brookings Institution, 1974).

48. Hamilton, S.B., Chavez, E.L. and Keilin, W.G. 'Thoughts on Armaggedon: the Relationship between Attitudes towards the Nuclear Threat and Cognitive/Emotional Responses', *International Journal of Mental Health*, 1986, vol. 15, no. 1, pp. 189–207.

49. Harris, R. *Gotcha! the Media, the Government and the Falklands Crisis* (London: Faber & Faber, 1983).

50. Haste, H. 'Adolescent Attitudes to the Nuclear Situation, and Appropriate Teaching Resources', paper given at Marc Goldstein Memorial Trust and MCANW Joint Conference, *Children in the Nuclear World: the Implications for Education*, 7 May 1988.

51. ———. 'Everybody's Scared – But Life Goes On: Coping, Defence and Activism in the Face of the Nuclear Threat', *Journal of Adolescence*, 1989, vol. 12, no. 1, pp. 11–26.

52. Hinde, Robert, 'Integrating Behavioural Sciences Against the Threat of War', *Medicine and War*, 1989, vol. 5, no. 1, p. 13.

53. Humphrey, Nicholas and Lifton, Robert J. (eds.) *In a Dark Time* (London: Faber & Faber, 1984).

54. Hunt, H., Munske, M., Orgel, M., Richman N. and Wason, A. 'Evaluation of the Effect of a Visit to the Soviet Union on London School Pupils' Attitudes, Knowledge, Hopes and Fears' (unpublished, 1988) SPINA, c/o MCANW, 601 Holloway Rd, London N19 4DJ.

55. Jones, S. and Saunders, H. *Growing Up in the Nuclear Age: an Interim Report of a Survey of Schoolchildren's Attitudes to Nuclear War* (Bristol: Bristol & Avon Peace Education Project, 1984).

56. Kovel, Joel, *Against the State of Nuclear Terror* (London: Pan, 1983).

57. Larkin, Philip, *Collected Poems* (London: Marvell Press and Faber & Faber, 1988).

58. L'Etang, H. *Fit to Lead?* (London: Heinemann, 1986).

59. Lifton, Robert J. *Death in Life. Survivors of Hiroshima* (New York: Basic Books, 1967).

60. ———. *The Broken Connection. On Death and the Continuity of Life*, Part III (New York: Basic Books, 1980).

61. ———, and Falk, Richard, *Indefensible Weapons. The Political and Psychological Case Against Nuclearism* (New York: Basic Books, 1982).

62. MacBride, S. *Many Voices, One World*. Report of the International Commission for the Study of Communication Problems (London: UNESCO, 1980).

63. Mack, J. Editorial Comment, *New England Journal of Medicine*, 1988, vol. 319, no. 7.

64. ———. 'The Threat of Nuclear War In Clinical Work', in *Psychoanalysis and the Nuclear Threat* (New Jersey: Analytic Press, 1988).

65. Macy, Joanna Rogers, *Despair and Personal Power in the Nuclear Age* (Philadelphia: New Society, 1983).

66. McGwire, M. 'Update: Soviet Military Objectives', *World Policy Journal*, 1987, vol. IV, no. 4.

67. McLean, Scilla (ed.) *How Nuclear Weapons Decisions Are Made* (Basingstoke: Macmillan, 1986).

68. Menzies, I.E.P. 'Thoughts on the Maternal Role in Contemporary Society', *Journal of Child Psychotherapy*, 1975, vol. 4, no. 1, pp. 5–14.

69. Miall, Hugh, *Nuclear Weapons – Who's in Charge?* (Basingstoke: Macmillan, 1987).

70. Miller, Alice, *For Your Own Good: The Roots of Violence in Child Rearing* (London: Virago, 1983).

71. ———. *Thou Shalt Not Be Aware: Society's Betrayal of the Child* (London: Pluto, 1985).

72. MORI/Independent, 'Hopes and Fears of Thatcher's Children', *Independent*, 3 May 1989.

73. Oliver, Pam, 'Survey of New Zealand Schoolchildren', *IPPNW New Zealand Affiliate Newsletter*, May 1989, p. 3.

74. Parens, Henri, 'Psychoanalytic Explorations of the Impact of the Threat of Nuclear Disaster on the Young', in Levine, H.B., Jacobs, O. and Rubin, C.J. (eds.) *Psychoanalysis and the Nuclear Threat: Clinical and Theoretical Studies* (New York: Analytic Press, 1987).

75. Oskamp, S. (ed.) International Conflict and National Public Policy Issues. *Applied Social Psychology Annual* (London: Society for the Psychological Study of Social Issues/Sage, 1985).

76. Palme, O. *Common Security: A Programme for Disarmament* (London: Pan, 1982).

77. Paulic, Breda, 'Mass Media Declaration and Disarmament', paper presented to UNESCO International Symposium on the Media and Disarmament, Nairobi, 1983.

78. Ponzo, E. *et al.* 'Italian Adolescents' Concerns about the Threat of Nuclear War', Proceedings of the International European Psychologists for Peace Conference, Helsinki, 1986.

79. Prins, G. (ed.) *The Choice: Nuclear Weapons Versus Security* (London: Chatto & Windus, 1984).

80. Public Agenda Foundation, *Voters' Options on Nuclear Arms Policy* (New York: Public Agenda Foundation, 1984).

81. Rapoport, Anatoli, 'International Relations and Game Theory', in Shaerf, C. and Barnaby, F.M. (eds.) *Disarmament and Arms Control* (New York: Gordon and Breach, 1972).

82. Rokeach, M. *Understanding Human Values* (New York: Free Press, 1979).

83. Royal Society, *Risk Assessment. A Study Group Report* (London: Royal Society, 1983).

84. Segal, Hanna, 'Review of "Against the State Of Nuclear Terror", Joel Kovel', *Free Associations*, 1987, no. 9, p. 139.

85. ——. 'Silence is the Real Crime', in Levine, H.B., Jacobs, O. and Rubin, C.J. (eds.) *Psychoanalysis and the Nuclear Threat: Clinical and Theoretical Studies* (New York: Analytic Press, 1988).

86. Simon, Herbert, *Administrative Behavior* (New York: Wiley, 1947).

87. Smoker, P. and Bradley, M. (eds.) *Special Issue on Accidental Nuclear War* (Tampere, Finland: Tampere Peace Research Institute, 1988).

88. Solantaus, Tytti, 'The Global World – A Domain for Development in Adolescence', *Journal of Adolescence*, 1989, vol. 12, no. 1, pp. 27–40.

89. ——. Rimpela, M. and Taipale, U. 'The Threat of War in the Minds of 12–18 year-olds in Finland', *Lancet*, 1984, vol. 8380, pp. 784–5.

90. Sommers, F.G., Goldberg, S. and Levinson, D. 'Children's Mental Health and the Threat of Nuclear War: a Canadian Pilot Study', in Solantaus, T., Chivian, E., Vartanyan, N. and Chihan, S. (eds.) *Impact of the Threat of Nuclear War on Children and Adolescents* (Boston: International Physicians for the Prevention of Nuclear War, 1985).

91. Steinbruner, John D. *The Cybernetic Theory of Decision. New Dimensions in Political Analysis* (Princeton: Princeton University Press, 1974).

92. Thomas, L.C. *Games, Theory and Applications* (Chichester: Wiley, 1984).

93. Thompson, James (ed.) *Psychological Aspects of Nuclear War. Statement of the British Psychological Society* (Chichester: Wiley, 1985).

94. Tizard, B. 'Old and New Paradigms: Research on Young People's Response to the Nuclear Threat', *Journal of Adolescence*, 1989, vol. 12, no. 1, pp. 1–10.

95. Trivers, R. *Social Evolution* (California: Benjamin Cummings, 1985).

96. U.S. Congressional Record. Hearings before the Committee on Armed Services, February, March 1983 (testimony of General Starry and Caspar Weinberger).

97. ——. The 600 Ship Navy and the Maritime Strategy (99th Congress, 1st Session) 24 June, 5, 6 and 10 September 1985 (testimony of Admiral James Watkins).

98. ——. Report of Defense Policy Panel (100th Congress), 13 September 1988, p. 10.

99. White, R. K. *Psychology and the Prevention of Nuclear War* (New York: University Press, 1986).

Videos

V1. Barnett, Lynn, *Enriching Day-care: a Comparison of Different Principles and Practices*, VHS, 38 minutes, 1989 (Concord Video & Film Council Ltd, 211 Felixstowe Rd, Ipswich IP3 9BJ).

V2. ——. *Everything's Going Berserk. Young Children Talk About the Nuclear Issue*, VHS, 17 minutes, colour, 1989 (Concord Video & Film Council).

V3. Williams, Pat, *Mum How Do You Spell Gorbatrof*, VHS, 46 minutes, 1986 (Australian Film Commission, available from MCANW).

MEDICAL CAMPAIGN against nuclear weapons

WHO WE ARE

The Medical Campaign Against Nuclear Weapons is an association of health care workers – such as doctors, nurses, psychologists, administrators, lab. technicians, social workers, therapists and students – who agree that the greatest threat to human health and welfare is nuclear weapons. They believe that preventing nuclear war is the only possible way to protect people from its medical consequences.

WHAT WE DO

The Medical Campaign provides information on the health implications of nuclear and chemical weapons, nuclear war and related issues. And we actively promote nuclear disarmament.

We do this by:
- Producing a range of materials including leaflets, posters, books and briefings
- Providing expert speakers for groups and for the media
- Attempting to influence decisions on nuclear weapons issues by lobbying Parliament, MPs and professional organisations
- Operating an information and briefing service for the media
- Organising national campaigns and conferences

JOIN US

☐ **I would like to join the Medical Campaign Against Nuclear Weapons**

NAME _____

JOB _____

HOME ADDRESS _____

_____

POSTCODE _____

PLACE OF WORK _____

TELEPHONE (HOME)_____

(WORK) _____

PROFESSIONAL ASSOCIATION OR TRADE UNION MEMBERSHIP_____

Subscription per year: £5 if annual income is less than £5,000; £10 if annual income is less than £10,000; £20 if annual income is more than £10,000; £30 if annual income is more than £20,000.

If you are not a health worker but would like to become a supporter of MCANW the subscription is £10 per year.

Please make your cheque payable to MCANW.

I enclose   £ _____ for my annual subscription

£ _____ further donation

☐ Please send me details of how to pay my subscription by Bankers Order

☐ Please send me details of the Medical Educational Trust (MET), a charity which supports MCANW's educational and information programmes

Return this form with your payment to:
Medical Campaign Against Nuclear Weapons
601 Holloway Road, London N19 4DJ.
Tel 01 272 2020